This book is dedicated to the
memory of Her Majesty Queen Mary,
whose love and appreciation of
fine jewels are reflected throughout
the royal collection.

HENRY VII *m.* Elizabeth of York
(1457–1509) (1466–1503)

HENRY VIII *m.* Catherine of Aragon *m.* Anne Boleyn *m.* Jane Seymour
(1491–1547) (1485–1536) (1st) (1507–1536) (2nd) (1509–1537) (3rd)

Margaret *m.* JAMES IV OF SCOTLAND
(1489–1541) (1473–1513)

Philip II of Spain *m.* MARY I
(1527–1598) (1516–1558)

ELIZABETH I
(1533–1603)

EDWARD VI
(1537–1553)

JAMES V OF SCOTLAND *m.* Mary of Guise
(1512–1542) (1515–1560)

MARY, QUEEN OF SCOTS *m.* Francis II of France *m.* Henry Stuart, Lord Darnley
(1542–1587) (1544–1560) (1st) (1545–1567) (2nd)

JAMES I *m.* Anne of Denma
(James VI of Scotland) (1574–1619)
(1566–1625)

Henry
(1594–1612)

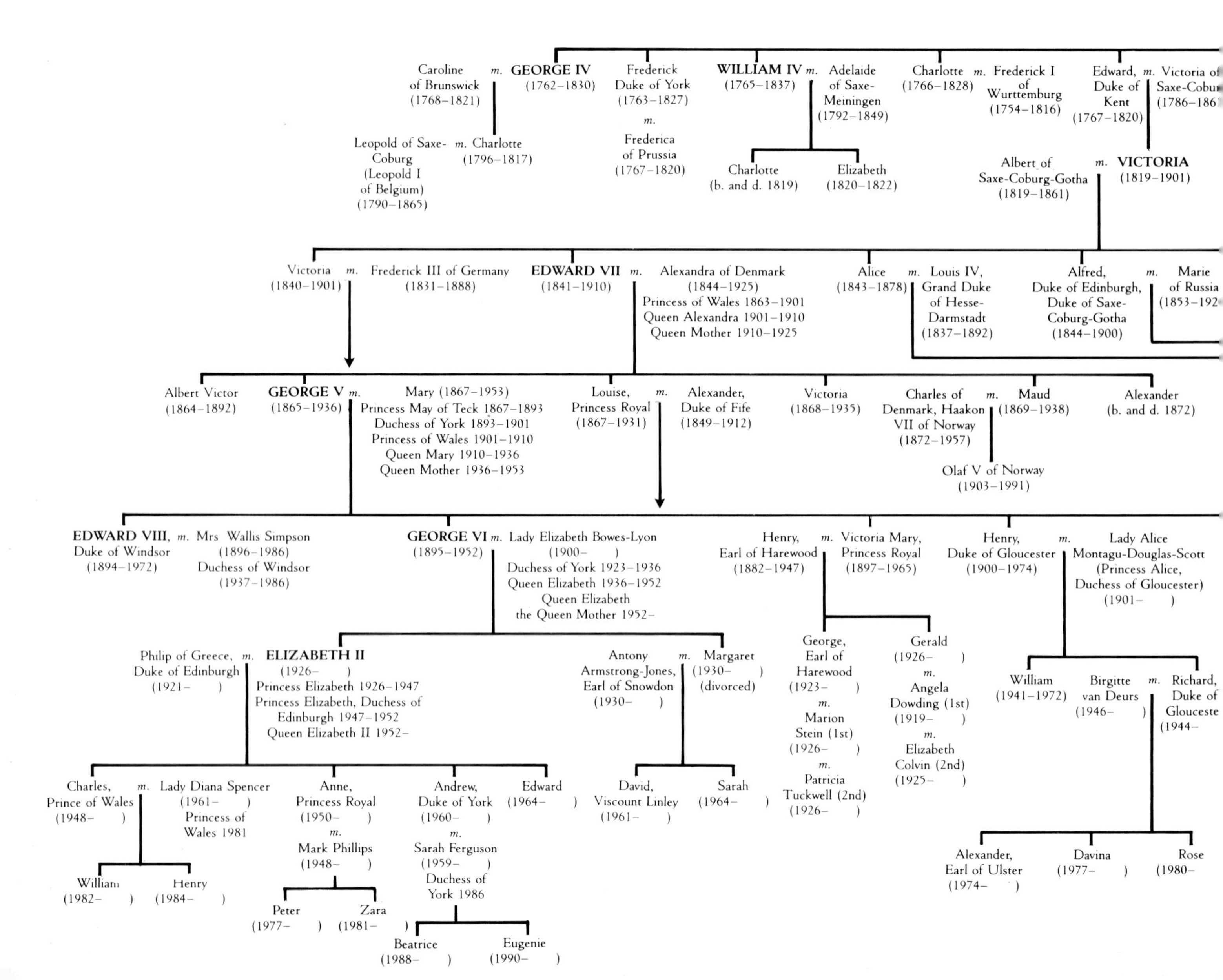

The Family Tree of Queen Elizabeth II

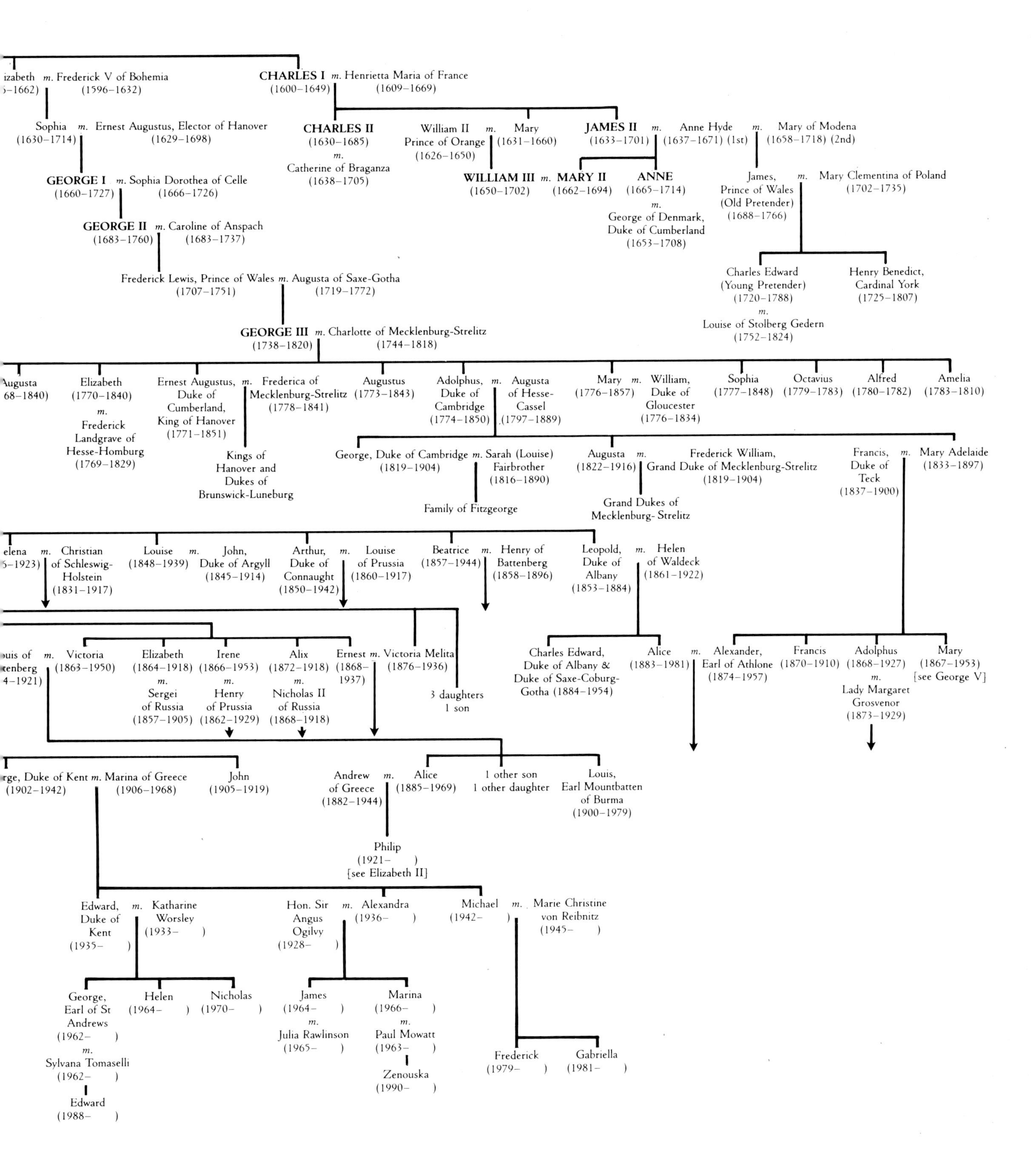

LESLIE FIELD

The JEWELS of QUEEN ELIZABETH II

HER PERSONAL COLLECTION

THAMES AND HUDSON

FRONTISPIECE: *Queen Mary's Kensington Bow Brooch*

Editor: Ruth A. Peltason

Designer: Dirk Luykx

First published in Great Britain in 1992 by Thames and Hudson Ltd, London

Concise, revised, paperback edition of *The Queen's Jewels*, published in 1987 by Harry N. Abrams, Inc., New York

Printed and bound in Japan

CONTENTS

TIARAS

EARRINGS

NECKLACES

BROOCHES

BRACELETS

WATCHES

RINGS

Acknowledgments

I WOULD LIKE TO ACKNOWLEDGE my deepest gratitude to Her Majesty the Queen for the help and guidance I have been given by Her Majesty's Household.

My grateful thanks to: Her Majesty Queen Elizabeth the Queen Mother; HRH the Duke of Edinburgh; HRH the Princess of Wales; HRH the Princess Anne, Mrs Mark Phillips; HRH the Princess Margaret, Countess of Snowdon; HRH Princess Alice, Duchess of Gloucester; HRH the Duchess of Gloucester; HRH the Duke of Kent; TRH Prince and Princess Michael of Kent; HRH Princess Alexandra, The Hon. Lady Ogilvy; The Earl of Harewood; The Marchioness of Cambridge; Lady May Abel Smith; and Lady Mary Whitley for their help and corrections.

I am especially grateful to Anne Neal, Marcus Bishop and Charles Noble for their assistance.

And my appreciation to all the following: Sir Alastair Aird, Joseph W. Allgood, George Anderson, Sandra Ankarcrona, Owen Arnot, John Asprey, Thomas Baring, Sir Simon Bland, Anne Beckwith-Smith, David Bennett, Pilar Boxford, Peter Brogan, J. Carter Brown, Sir Richard Buckley, Joan Burgoyne, Teresa Buxton, Amar Singh Chhatwal, David Chipp, Daniel Cleary, Sir Robert Cooke, Tim Cooper, David Cottingham, Elizabeth Cuthbert, Terence Davidson, Gilbert de Botton, Damon de Laszlo, Patrick de Laszlo, Frances Dimond, Michael Doran, Allan Douglas, Michael Dover, Cedric Evans, David Evans, Oliver Everett, Colonel Michael Farmer, The Rt. Hon. Sir Robert Fellowes, Maurice Foster, Susie Friend, Margaret Godfrey, Paul Gottlieb, Gerald Grant, John Haslam, Sally Hine, Brenda Hodgson, Jennie Holden, Peter Hubble, Helen Hughes, Caroline and Anwar Hussein, Robin Janvrin, Tim Jenkins, Geoff Katz, Amanda Kiddy, The Hon. Lady King, Fiona Koops, Ed and Julie Kosner, Laurence Krashes, Andreas Landshoff, Jane Langton, Carol Lemon, Sarah Lindsay, John Lloyd-Morgan, Felicity Luard, Fiona Lukes, Dirk Luykx, Barbara Lyons, Major-General Patrick MacLellan, Alistair S. McDavid, The Hon. Diana Makgill, Anthony Marangos, Paul Marmin, Brigadier Kenneth Mears, Marilyn Meyers, Mona Mitchell, Geoffrey C. Munn, Hans Nadelhoffer, Lord Napier and Ettrick, Cecilia Neal, Carley Newman, Nicholas Norton, Michael O'Mara, Anthony Oppenheimer, Lady Angela Oswald, Michael Oswald, Byron Ousey, Fred Parkes, John Partridge, Ruth Peltason, Terence Pepper, Mark Piel, Leslie Ricketts, Liz Robbins, Daniel Roger, Kenneth Rose, John Sandoe, Hans Schnepper, Fiona Shakerley, Sir Geoffrey Shakerley, The Hon. Frances Shand Kydd, Michael Shea, John Shelley, Francesca Sherwood, David V. Thomas, James Todd, Heinrich Graf von Spreti, Clodagh Waddington, Robin D. G. Walker, Anne Wall, Philip Ward-Jackson, David Warren, Sir Francis Watson, Roger Wemyss-Brooks, The Hon. Jessica White, Patricia White, Marjorie Willis, Ronald Winston, Caroline Zubaida.

INTRODUCTION

MY FASCINATION WITH THE ROYAL JEWELS goes back to my earliest childhood and was inextricably linked to the glamourous fairy tale appeal of the monarchy. I started work researching the subject of the royal jewels in 1980 and I had to sift through 450,000 photographs in order to compile a twelve-volume inventory of every jewel ever owned by any living member of the royal family. I read long-forgotten memoirs, royal diaries and biographies, and checked crumbling old newspapers and periodicals. I was surprised to find how many pieces have survived from the eighteenth century and the early Hanoverian monarchs. It was interesting to trace changes in taste and fashion while examining pictures of seven generations of the royal family wearing the same jewels. And I realized that this is not a moribund museum collection, but that the royal jewels have been worn, possibly redesigned, and then worn again according to each owner's taste and needs.

Last July I attended the first royal garden party of the season. It was a blazingly hot summer day and the usually green springy lawn of Buckingham Palace was baked hard and looked parched and dry. Even on such a memorable occasion I constantly circled amongst my fellow guests, obsessed with seeing what jewels the Queen, the Princess of Wales, the Princess Royal and Princess Alexandra would be wearing. To my great delight and unutterable satisfaction Her Majesty was wearing the splendid diamond and pearl brooch that I had christened in 1987 'The Duchess of Teck's Corsage Brooch' and which I had been able to trace back to her great grandmother.

If I try to remember now my first glimpses of royal jewels, multiple images spring to mind. The astonishing size and weight of the pear-shaped pendant diamond earrings worn by Queen Elizabeth the Queen Mother at a St James's Palace reception; the bright vivid hue of an enormous sapphire brooch pinned to the Queen's suit on a visit to the Courtauld Institute of Art in Portman Square; the blurred movement of the charms swinging from Princess Alexandra's gold link bracelet at a lunch in a Pall Mall club; the staggering turquoise and diamond parure the Duchess of Gloucester wore at a Government House reception in Melbourne, Australia; the two lustrous rows of pearls around the Queen's neck at a drinks party Prince Philip gave for Bing Crosby at Buckingham Palace; and finally the overwhelming size of a pearl and diamond pendant brooch that I admired at an earlier garden party.

After the publication of *The Queen's Jewels* in 1987 my interest if anything intensified, and I was overwhelmed by the letters that arrived from around the world, from people whose knowledge was remarkable and encyclopedic. With this new edition of the book I wanted to put together all the tiaras or brooches or bracelets so that they could be more easily compared. It is fascinating to see the differences in style between the four diamond bows; or to discover how much more delicate Edwardian design is than Victorian. All the jewellery in this book has been inherited by the Queen or given to her as family gifts from her parents and her husband. But as the Queen is a link in a chain of historical continuity I've also shown jewels that she has given or loaned to her daughter and two daughters-in-law.

It may seem surprising that a woman with such a stupendous collection of jewels is given still more, but when the Queen launches a ship, opens a factory or makes a State visit the event is often marked by the presentation of a valuable piece of jewellery and such a gift becomes her private property.

There have been ridiculous estimates of the value of the Queen's jewels, but it truly is incalculable because of its royal provenance dating back to the sixteenth century. Many of the gems came from foreign lands and have sometimes arrived in Britain as the unlooked-for result of such shattering events as civil wars, deaths or revolutions.

Although I have seen numerous widely varying estimates as to the size of the collection, there is no complete inventory, whether official or unofficial. But the catalogue I have compiled shows that the Queen owns, or has worn–and these are not quite the same thing as some pieces have never been worn, while others were loaned to her when she was young by Queen Elizabeth the Queen Mother–fourteen tiaras, thirty-seven pairs of earrings, one hundred and five brooches, fifty-eight necklaces, thirty-seven bracelets, six pendants, fourteen watches and fifteen rings.

When the childless King William IV died on 20 June 1837 he was succeeded by his niece. The Crown Regalia is the property of the State, but Queen Victoria inherited in her own right the family collection of jewels, which included pearls bought by Queen Elizabeth I and diamonds that had belonged to King George III. During the sixty-four years of Queen Victoria's reign her collection of jewels probably increased ten-fold. Royal wills are never made public so exactly how she divided her vast private fortune among her descendants cannot be known for certain. However her will included a schedule of jewels that were to be considered 'as belonging to the Crown and to be worn by all future Queens in right of it'.

Queen Victoria's beautiful daughter-in-law, the Danish Princess Alexandra, was fifty-seven when she became Queen Consort on the accession of King Edward VII, and she personified the glamour of the Edwardian era. She had been Princess of Wales for thirty-seven years from 1863 to 1901. She was Queen Consort for nine years from 1901 to 1910 and then Queen Mother from 1910 until her death on 20 November 1925. Queen Alexandra epitomized the popular concept of a queen clothed in a shimmering haze of precious gems. When she entered Westminster Abbey for her Coronation on 9 August 1902 one spectator reported that she looked as if she was 'ablaze with light'.

Her successor, Princess May of Teck, was born at Kensington Palace on 26 May 1867. In 1893 she married Queen Alexandra's second son, the Duke of York. She was Duchess of York until 1901 when she succeeded her mother-in-law as Princess of Wales. In 1910 Princess May's husband became King George V and she became Queen Mary. After King George V's death in 1936 Queen Mary was Queen Mother until her own death on 24 March 1953.

'Ablaze, regal and overpowering', she personified the traditional splendour of the monarchy, and amassed a greater collection of priceless jewellery than any previous Queen of England. One of her contemporaries wrote in 1936 shortly before King George died: 'I have never known any Empress or Queen who could wear a quantity of superb jewels with such ease and simplicity and without appearing in the least overladen'.

King George VI succeeded his brother King Edward VIII in December 1936. The new Queen had been Lady Elizabeth Bowes-Lyon until her marriage in 1923 to the Duke of York. She was Duchess of York until her husband's accession when she became Queen Consort. Since King George VI's death on 6 February 1952 she has been known as Queen Elizabeth the Queen Mother.

Jewels are an important part of the royal image and on State occasions the Queen has a duty to be regal, for these events are part of the national heritage and there is splendour and glory in their observance. Pageantry is an indispensable part of royalty; and one of the joys of monarchy is the spectacle we associate with it. The royal jewels are above fashion and beyond price.

The Queen principally wears jewellery that belonged to her ancestors but she has added modern pieces to the royal collection, so that decades from now her descendants will wear designs created during her reign. The royal jewels are historically important and reinforce the sense of stability that is the British monarchy's greatest strength. The Queen lives in Windsor Castle, which has been a stronghold of the monarchy for nearly one thousand years. She travels to ceremonial occasions in horse-drawn carriages that date back hundreds of years. Yet perhaps the strongest chain of family continuity is forged by the personal collection of jewels that she wears, appreciates and of which she is lifelong custodian.

LESLIE FIELD
London, 1991

THE KING GEORGE III FRINGE TIARA

The diamond fringe tiara – a graduated circle of vertical rows of diamonds – was made in 1830 as a necklace from brilliant-cut stones that had belonged to King George III (page 12). Although designed to be worn either as a collar or mounted on a thin wire band as a tiara, it is as a necklace that its sunray design is most apparent. Queen Victoria first wore it as a tiara when she paid an official visit to the Opera in 1839. ABOVE: *In Winterhalter's painting* The First of May, *done in 1851, she wears it as she holds Prince Arthur, the future Duke of Connaught, while his godfather the Duke of Wellington presents him with a jewel-studded gold box and Prince Albert looks on. In her will,*

the necklace was one of the items Queen Victoria left to the Crown, and it was then described as a diamond fringe necklace. OPPOSITE, ABOVE LEFT: *It was inherited by Queen Mary when she became Queen Consort in 1910, and she in turn gave it to her daughter-in-law the new Queen in 1937.* OPPOSITE, ABOVE RIGHT: *When Queen Elizabeth, now the Queen Mother, first appeared in it at the Duchess of Sutherland's Coronation Ball at Hampden House, MP 'Chips' Channon noted disparagingly in his diary that she wore white, and 'an ugly spiked tiara'. She wears it here in 1953.* OPPOSITE, BELOW LEFT: *She loaned it as the 'something borrowed' to her daughter Princess Elizabeth for her wedding in 1947. As the Princess was getting dressed in her second-floor room at Buckingham Palace before leaving for Westminster Abbey, the frame snapped and the court jeweller, who was standing by in case of any emergency, rushed to his workroom with a police escort. Queen Elizabeth reassured her nervous daughter that it could be repaired in time, and it was.* OPPOSITE, BELOW RIGHT: *Queen Elizabeth the Queen Mother loaned it again to her granddaughter Princess Anne for her marriage to Captain Mark Phillips in 1973. The Princess wore with it the diamond flower-cluster earrings that had been a wedding gift from her mother, the Queen.*

QUEEN MARY'S 'GIRLS OF GREAT BRITAIN AND IRELAND' TIARA

In 1893 a committee was formed by Lady Eve Greville to raise money from the 'Girls of Great Britain and Ireland' to purchase a wedding gift for Princess May of Teck, the future Queen Mary. They collected more than £5,000, and after buying a diamond tiara from Garrard, the surplus money was given, at Princess May's request, to a fund that had just been set up to aid the widows and orphans of the men lost after the sinking of HMS Victoria. *In her thank-you letter, dated 4 July 1893, Princess May wrote:*

'I need scarcely assure you that the tiara will ever be one of my most valued wedding gifts as a precious proof of your goodwill and affection.'

The tiara was a diamond festoon-and-scroll design surmounted by nine large oriental pearls on diamond spikes and set on a bandeau base of alternate round and lozenge collets between two plain bands of diamonds.

Alice Hughes

PAGE 15, ABOVE LEFT: *Queen Mary, then Duchess of York, wearing the tiara shortly after her marriage. The ornate diamond and pearl necklace, which could also be worn as a tiara, was another wedding gift, presented by 'Some Ladies of England'.* PAGE 15, ABOVE RIGHT: *By 1920 Queen Mary had removed the bandeau base and the upright pearls, replacing them with large collet diamonds. This photograph was taken in 1930.* PAGE 15, BELOW: *Around 1921 she wore the bandeau as a simple headband.* PAGE 14: *This is how the tiara looked in 1947 when Queen Mary gave it to the Queen, then Princess Elizabeth, as a wedding present. Its broken spiky line emphasized by diamond collets, the tiara has the great advantage of being exceptionally lightweight. At the exhibition of 2,660 wedding gifts held in the State Apartments of St James's Palace and opened to the public in aid of charity, the tiara and the bandeau were displayed separately on curved velvet stands.* ABOVE, RIGHT: *This photograph taken in 1949 shows the Queen wearing her first tiara, which she still affectionately calls 'Granny's Tiara'. She is also wearing the smallest watch in the world, made by Cartier. The dial measured only 3/16 inch across and was set in a bracelet of thirty-two miniature platinum squares. Her father and mother, on a State visit to France in 1938, accepted it on her behalf from the President of the French Republic, Monsieur Lebrun, as a gift from the French people. Princess Elizabeth was then twelve years old. She wore it almost daily – even at her wedding and Coronation – until 13 January 1955 when she lost it while out walking the dogs at Sandringham. Despite an intensive search by the police, farm workers, Boy Scouts and even soldiers with mine detectors, it was never found. In 1957, when she herself made a State visit to France, the Government presented her with a replacement that was nearly as small, only this one was set in a diamond and platinum bracelet strap. This photograph also records one of the rare times that Her Majesty wore coloured nail varnish.* ABOVE, LEFT: *In 1969 the Queen had the bandeau and the tiara reassembled, as is seen here in 1981 at the Royal Variety Performance.*

Princess Andrew of Greece's Meander Tiara

The word 'meander' derives from the River Maiandros, which in ancient Greece inspired a classical design of regular lines set at right angles to each other that was often used both in architecture and works of art. It began to be popular in modern jewellery design around the turn of the century. The design is commonly known as the key pattern, which is how Prince Philip says he has always known this tiara. This meander tiara also incorporates a central wreath of leaves and scrolls on either side. It was a wedding gift to the Queen from her mother-in-law, Princess Andrew of Greece, born Princess Alice of Battenberg, Queen Victoria's great-granddaughter. The Queen has never worn it in public and gave it to Princess Anne around 1972. Princess Anne wears it here in 1973 with her diamond and sapphire engagement ring and a diamond brooch – a six-pointed star with diamond collets that she received when she launched HMNZS Canterbury *at the Yarrow shipyard in 1970.*

Queen Alexandra's Russian Kokoshnik Tiara and Queen Mary's Floret Earrings

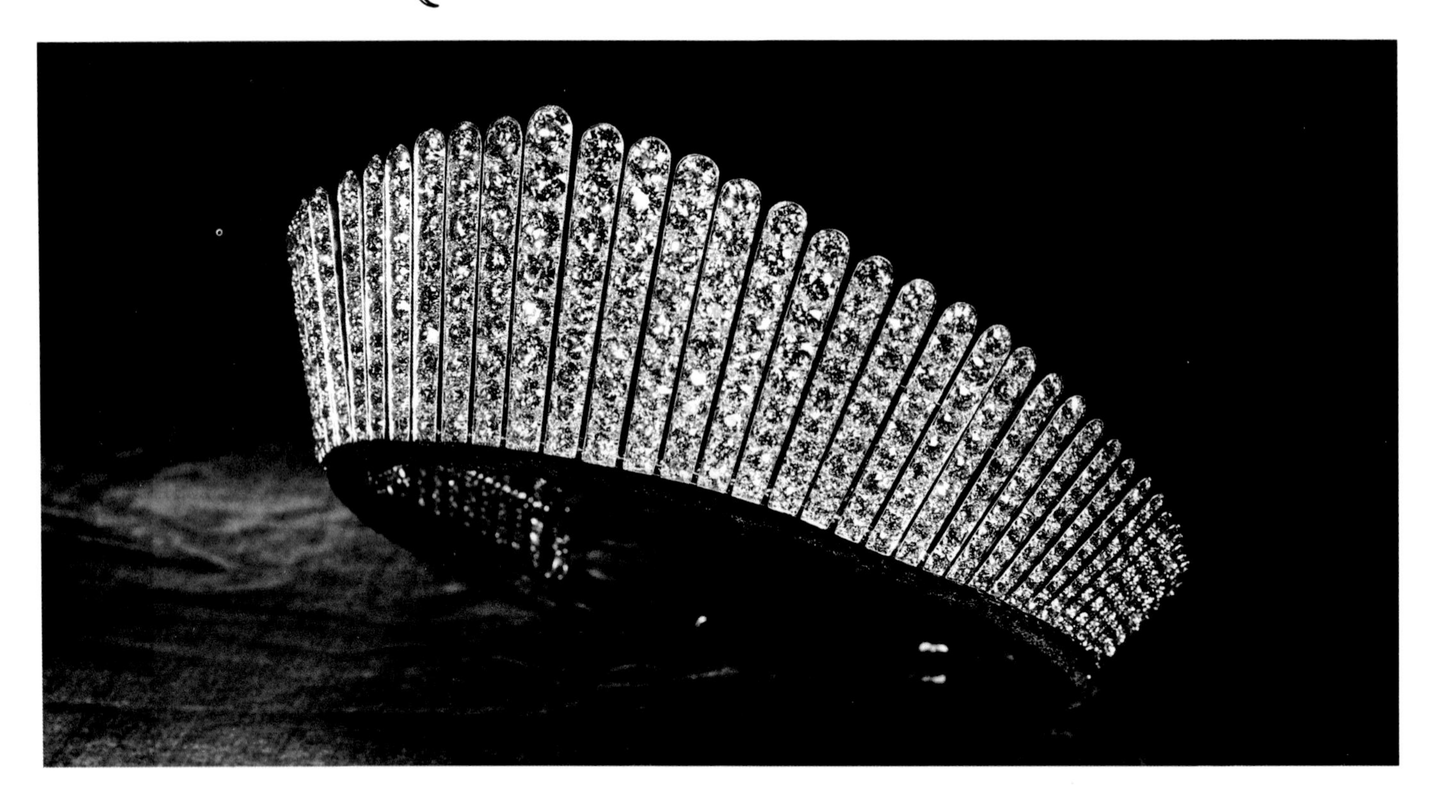

OPPOSITE, ABOVE: *On 10 March 1888 the Prince and Princess of Wales celebrated their silver wedding anniversary at Marlborough House. Before they hosted a large family dinner party, Princess Alexandra received Lady Salisbury, who presented her with this diamond tiara on behalf of 365 peeresses of the United Kingdom. As Princess May wrote to her Aunt Augusta, the Grand Duchess of Mecklenburg-Strelitz:*

*'The presents are quite magnificent.
The ladies of society gave a lovely diamond spiked tiara.'*

Princess Alexandra had specially requested that the tiara be in the fashionable Russian style of a peasant girl's headdress; she knew the Kokoshnik *design well because her sister, the Empress of Russia, had an identical one. The tiara was made by Garrard, supervised by the Marchionesses of Ailesbury and Salisbury and the Countesses of Cork and Spencer. It is formed of sixty-one platinum bars graduating from the centre in the eighteenth-century manner and totally encrusted with 488 diamonds, of which the two biggest are 3.25 carats each.* OPPOSITE, BELOW: *These floret earrings have a large centre diamond surrounded by seven slightly smaller ones and were bought by Queen Mary.* ABOVE, LEFT: *Queen Alexandra in 1893 at the wedding of the Duke of York and Princess May of Teck. The elaborate diamond and pearl necklace she is wearing beneath the rows of chokers was her wedding present from the Prince of Wales in 1863, but here she has attached additional pendant drops which come from another necklace she later wore at her 1902 coronation. Queen Elizabeth the Queen Mother currently wears the necklace in its original design (page 92).* ABOVE, RIGHT: *Queen Mary in the official portrait to celebrate her eightieth birthday on 26 May 1947 is also wearing Queen Alexandra's diamond* collier résille *made by Cartier in 1904 (page 76, above right).* RIGHT: *The Queen photographed in the Blue Drawing Room of Buckingham Palace in 1961.*

Queen Elizabeth the Queen Mother's Halo Scroll Tiara

ABOVE, LEFT: *The halo design scroll tiara was bought from Cartier by the Duchess of York in August 1936, and is set with 1,311 brilliant and baton cut diamonds. This photograph, with the Duke, was taken just weeks before King Edward VIII's abdication. Queen Elizabeth still wears the diamond and pearl drop earrings, which she has had since shortly after her marriage. The diamond tiara, with its fan-shaped motifs, was given to the Queen, but she has never worn it in public.* ABOVE, RIGHT: *She loaned it for a number of years to her sister, Princess Margaret, seen here in 1962, and then to her daughter, Princess Anne, who wore it for this 1973 portrait by William Narraway (left).*

The Cambridge Lover's Knot Tiara

One of the most charming tributes that Queen Mary ever paid to the maternal side of her family was the tiara that she had made by Garrard in 1914 to her own design and from pearls and diamonds already in her possession. It was a copy of one owned by her grandmother, Princess Augusta of Hesse, who married the first Duke of Cambridge, seventh son of King George III, in 1818. She had been given it by her family prior to her marriage. There was a strong French influence in its neo-classical design of nineteen openwork diamond arches, each enclosing an oriental pearl drop from a diamond lover's knot bow, and surmounted by single diamonds and upright oval pearl spikes. Princess Augusta's tiara was set on a circular band of perfectly matched pearls, but Queen Mary chose a base of diamonds for hers. In the nineteenth century it was a popular design and there are five known versions still in existence. When the Duchess of Cambridge's eldest daughter, and namesake, Augusta, married the Grand Duke of Mecklenburg-Strelitz in 1843, she gave her the tiara as a wedding present. The Grand Duchess, in turn, became godmother, and ultimately closest confidante, to her niece, the future Queen Mary, who saw her annually and knew the tiara well. In 1912 she wrote to her aunt:

'If you have a dinner to celebrate yr birthday you must wear on yr 90th birthday the pearl & diamond diadem & yr English orders, do please do so for my sake. Think how beautiful you will look with yr white hair and still lovely neck.'

PAGE 21: *Queen Mary's tiara as seen today with the upright pearl spikes removed.* OPPOSITE, ABOVE LEFT: *The Duchess of Cambridge wearing her tiara at the time of her marriage in 1818.* OPPOSITE, ABOVE RIGHT: *The Grand Duchess of Mecklenburg-Strelitz in the 1890s. She is also wearing the necklace from the 'Cambridge sapphires' parure (page 76, below left).* OPPOSITE, BELOW LEFT: *Queen Mary in 1926, wearing the tiara as originally made.* OPPOSITE, BELOW RIGHT: *By 1935 she had removed the upright pearls and is wearing four of them as pendants on her ropes of pearls. She gave her pearl and diamond dog-collar to Princess Alice, Duchess of Gloucester, who has now passed it on to her daughter-in-law, the present Duchess.* RIGHT: *In her will, Queen Mary left the tiara to the Queen, who wears it in 1955. In 1981 the Queen gave it to the Princess of Wales as a wedding present, who wore it for the first time at the State Opening of Parliament that November.* BELOW: *In 1985 the Princess wore the tiara and pearl and diamond drop earrings, which had been a wedding gift from the jewellers Collingwood, on her official visit to Washington.*

The Grand Duchess Vladimir of Russia's Tiara

At the beginning of the twentieth century the Grand Duke Vladimir Alexandrovitch, son of Tsar Alexander II, brother of Tsar Alexander III and uncle of Tsar Nicholas II, was the richest and most influential aristocrat in Russia. Artistic and clever, in 1874 he had married the twenty-year-old German Princess Marie von Mecklenburg-Schwerin, who bore the Russian name of Marie Pavlovna, although she was known as 'Miechen' because there were so many other Grand Duchess Maries in the family. The Empress Alexandra was agonizingly shy, uninterested in society and totally engrossed in her family, so the Grand Duchess Vladimir became the leading hostess in St Petersburg and set up an alternative Court in her magnificent Vladimir Palace on the Neva river. Her collection of jewels nearly equalled that of the Dowager Empress Marie Feodorovna, and in the Russian style they were displayed to her guests. When the Duchess of Marlborough, American-born Consuelo Vanderbilt, visited St Petersburg in 1902, she wrote in her diary:

'After dinner the Grand Duchess showed me her jewels set out in glass cases in her dressing-room. There were endless parures *of diamonds, emeralds, rubies and pearls, to say nothing of semi-precious stones such as turquoises, tourmalines, cat's eyes and aquamarines.'*

ABOVE: *In the 1880s, the Grand Duchess commissioned a Russian jeweller to make her a diamond tiara of fifteen interlaced circles, with a swinging oriental pearl suspended in each. In 1911 she left the tiara in Cartier's Paris workroom for cleaning, and while this was being done they took the opportunity of making at least three copies, which later led to the mistaken assumption that Cartier had designed the original as well.*

The Grand Duke had died in 1908, and at the time of the Russian Revolution, in 1917, the Grand Duchess moved with her retinue of servants and ladies-in-waiting to Kislovodsk in the Caucasus, which was still in the hands of loyal Cossack troops. Towards the end of 1919 she made her escape by horse-drawn carriage and train, finally settling in Zurich. She had taken a case of jewels with her when she left St Petersburg, but the bulk of her collection had been left walled up in a hidden safe in the Vladimir Palace. Before the war one of her protégés had been a young Englishman called the Hon. Albert (Bertie) Stopford, who was attached to the British Embassy working for the Secret Intelligence Service. He managed to stay in touch with her in Kislovodsk, and once she was safely abroad, he enlisted the help of one of her loyal elderly retainers to get him into the sacked Palace at night. The looters had not discovered the secret safe and he was able to remove the jewels, dividing them into the smallest possible pieces before wrapping them in newspapers and packing them into two shabby leather Gladstone bags.

According to the Countess of Airlie, Queen Mary's lady-in-waiting and closest confidante, Stopford actually disguised himself as an old woman and hid this tiara in the lining of his black bonnet, cramming the fifteen pearl drops into cherries that were sewn on as trimming. Whether this part of the story is true or not most certainly Stopford managed to get all the jewels out of Russia, possibly using diplomatic channels to do so. On 6 September 1920 the Grand Duchess died while staying in the French spa of Contrexéville. Her jewels were divided among her four children: the emeralds went to Grand Duke Boris, the pearls to Grand Duke Cyril, the rubies to Grand Duke Andrei, and the diamonds to her only daughter, the Grand Duchess Helen, who in 1902 had married Prince Nicholas of Greece, the third son of King George I and Queen Olga. OPPOSITE, BELOW: *In 1921, Queen Mary bought the tiara from Princess Nicholas who had settled in Paris with her husband and three daughters, one of whom was Princess Marina, the future Duchess of Kent. Queen Mary had the last fifteen of the Cambridge emeralds mounted as drops so that they could be interchanged with the pearls (page 51).* ABOVE: *The Queen inherited the tiara in 1953. She is photographed in 1959 on the Grand Staircase of Buckingham Palace. Her pearl studs were made in 1951.*

The Queen's Pear Drop Earrings

LEFT: *These modern, gold-set diamond stud earrings with large pear-shaped drops were made from family stones.* BELOW, LEFT: *The Queen and Prince Philip at a film premiere in 1968.* BELOW, RIGHT: *In 1983 the Queen loaned the earrings to the Princess of Wales who was making her first official visit to Australia. At a banquet she wore the earrings with the Spencer family diamond tiara and the string of pearls with a diamond and sapphire clasp she received as a wedding present.*

THE GREVILLE CHANDELIER EARRINGS AND KING GEORGE VI FESTOON NECKLACE

ABOVE: *These long Cartier chandelier earrings ending in three drops show examples of every known modern cut of diamond. They were a wedding gift to Princess Elizabeth in 1947 from her parents. Queen Elizabeth had inherited them from the Hon. Mrs Ronnie Greville in 1942. Princess Elizabeth was unable to wear them until she had her ears pierced. When it was noticed that she had done so, doctors and jewellers found themselves inundated with women anxious to have their ears pierced as well.* ABOVE, RIGHT: *In 1947 King George wanted to make some jewellery from 239 loose diamond collets that he had inherited, and in 1950 105 of them were set in this three-row festoon necklace with triangle motifs.* RIGHT: *In 1962 the Queen attended a Gilbert and Sullivan gala wearing the earrings and necklace.*

Queen Mary's Cluster Earrings

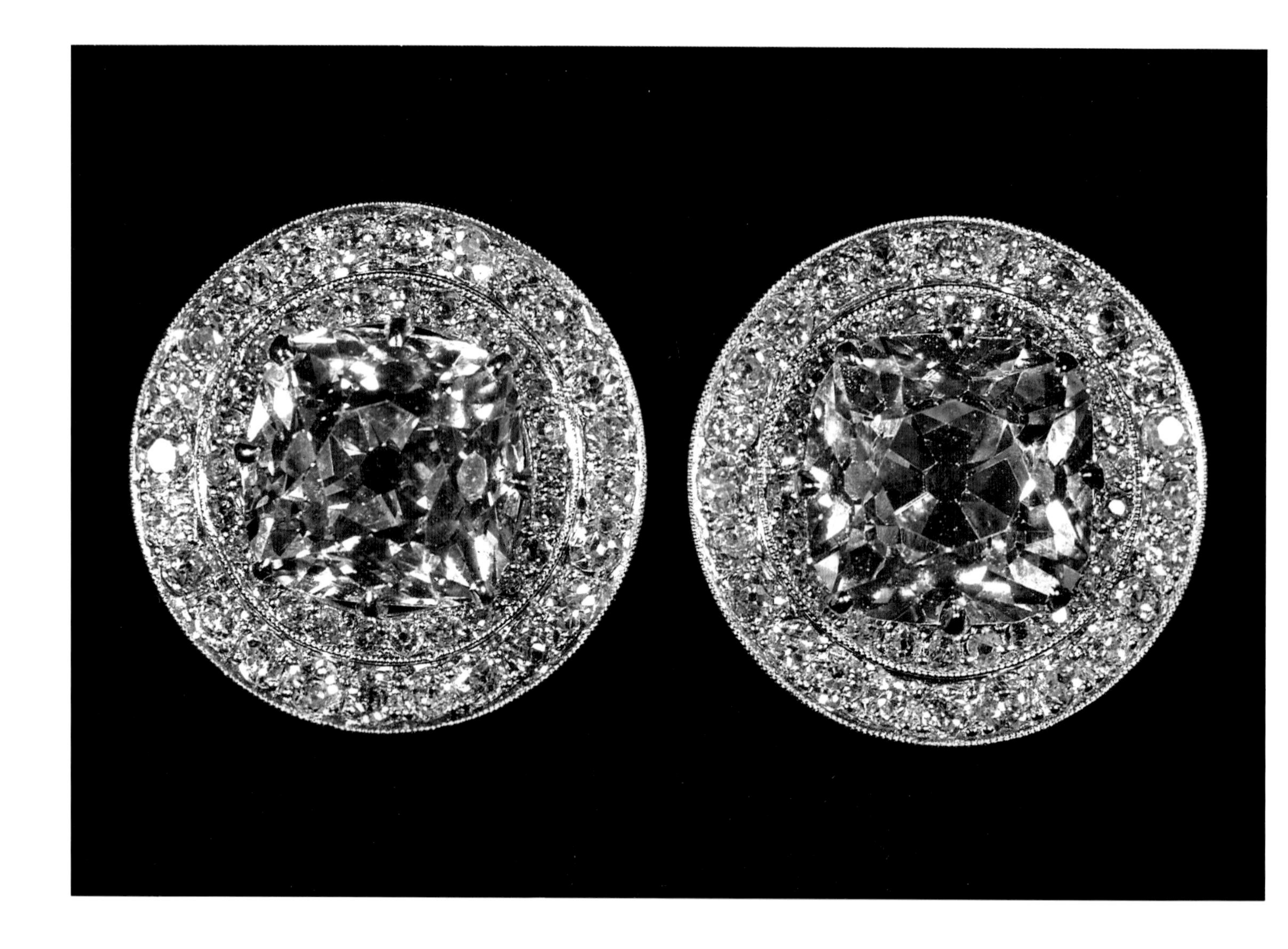

ABOVE: *Each of these unusual earrings has a large, brilliant-cut diamond sunk into two concentric circles of small diamonds set in platinum with a millegrain edge.* OPPOSITE, LEFT: *Queen Mary wore the earrings in 1948. Her diamond cluster brooch with a pearl centre was left to Princess Alice, Duchess of Gloucester, and is now worn as the centrepiece of a four-row pearl necklace by her daughter-in-law, the present Duchess.* OPPOSITE, RIGHT: *The Queen, in 1953, making her Christmas broadcast from Auckland, New Zealand, during her six-month-long Coronation tour of the Commonwealth. She is also wearing the necklace and bracelet made from her very first diamonds. In 1947 King George VI and Queen Elizabeth took their daughters to South Africa on a post-war tour, to express their appreciation to the people who had fought so valiantly. Princess Elizabeth's*

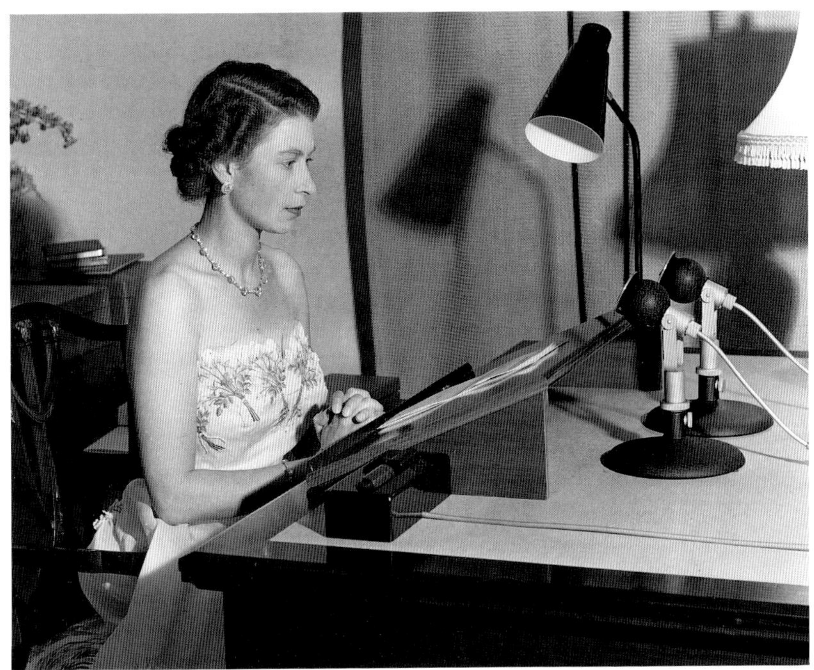

birthday, 21 April, was declared a public holiday throughout the Union of South Africa and that night a Young People's Ball was given in her honour at Government House in Cape Town. The King and Queen did their best to stay in the background as, dressed in a white tulle evening gown sparkling with diamanté and sequin embroidery, Princess Elizabeth was presented by Field-Marshal Smuts with her gift from the Government: a silver casket containing a long chain necklace of twenty-one large diamonds that had been cut and polished in Johannesburg, the largest of which was 10 carats. Forming connecting links between each of the twenty-one main stones were two small brilliant-cut diamonds mounted on either side of a baguette diamond. The casket was handed to Princess Elizabeth as she stood by a microphone and the entire nation heard her gasp of delight when she saw the necklace. From that night on, she has always called them 'my best diamonds'. Five years later, shortly after the Queen acceded to the throne, she decided to have the necklace shortened and it was cut down to fifteen large stones, the other six with their connecting links being made up into a matching bracelet. During their South African tour, the royal family had visited the Big Hole, the first and greatest of the Kimberley diamond mines, and the Princess had been given a superb round-cut, 6-carat, blue-white diamond, presented by little Mary Oppenheimer, daughter of the Chairman of the De Beers Corporation. In 1952 this stone was added as a centrepiece to the new bracelet. The Queen has continued to wear the set throughout the years, from her eve-of-wedding ball at Buckingham Palace to the Royal Opera House gala to celebrate her sixtieth birthday in 1986.

Queen Victoria's Stud Earrings

ABOVE: *Two perfectly matched, large, brilliant-cut diamonds, which Queen Victoria had set as ear studs.* OPPOSITE, ABOVE LEFT: *She wore them in this portrait taken in 1873 when she was fifty-four. The huge diamond set in the brooch on the bodice of her dress is the 106-carat Koh-I-Noor.* OPPOSITE, ABOVE RIGHT: *Queen Alexandra in 1901.* OPPOSITE, BELOW LEFT: *Queen Mary in 1950. The oval brooch set with diamonds pinned to her collar belonged to Empress Marie Feodorovna of Russia before the turn of the century, when it also had three large oval diamond drops. Queen Mary bought it from her estate in 1929, and on her death in 1953 left it to Princess Marina, Duchess of Kent. It now belongs to Princess Michael of Kent.* OPPOSITE, BELOW RIGHT: *The Queen in 1961, visiting Freetown, Sierra Leone. Her modern gold brooch set with pavé diamonds has seven curved sprays of baguette diamonds and an arc of graduated square rubies. Her four-row necklace was made from family pearls.*

The Duchess of Teck's Earrings

QUEEN VICTORIA'S DROP EARRINGS

OPPOSITE, ABOVE LEFT: *These perfectly matched pearl earrings are each surrounded by eight diamonds. They were a twentieth-birthday present to the Queen from her grandmother, Queen Mary, who had inherited them in 1897 on the death of her mother, Princess Mary Adelaide, Duchess of Teck. The Queen wore them for her wedding, and until she had her ears pierced and could wear the many others she owned, they were seen constantly, and have been seen as recently as 1984 when she visited Canada.* OPPOSITE, BELOW LEFT: *Princess Mary Adelaide, Duchess of Teck in 1883.* OPPOSITE, ABOVE RIGHT: *Queen Mary in 1910. She is also wearing one of the black enamel and diamond mourning brooches made to observe the death of King Edward VII. Queen Alexandra had an identical brooch. Both Queen Mary and her mother had pierced ears, but clip-on backs were added to the earrings when they were given to the Queen.* OPPOSITE, BELOW RIGHT: *The Queen and Prince Philip four days after their wedding in 1947. In addition to the earrings, she is wearing a double string of pearls, which her parents had given her during the war, and a platinum-set chrysanthemum brooch with sapphire stamens and diamond petals and stem, which had been a gift from Sir John Laing and Sons Ltd and the Anglo-Iranian Oil Company Ltd when she launched the oil tanker* British Princess *at Sunderland in 1946.*

ABOVE, LEFT: *In 1838, when she was nineteen, Queen Victoria was drawn by Richard James Lane, wearing a pair of pearl drop earrings. In 1847, Prince Albert gave her another, similar pair, but with larger pear-shaped pearls, each hung from a diamond stud from the royal collection. When she died she left them to the Crown.* ABOVE, RIGHT: *The Queen is wearing them for the annual Garter ceremony at St George's Chapel, Windsor, in 1954.*

Queen Alexandra's Cluster Earrings

ABOVE, TOP: *These large pearl earrings, each surrounded by ten diamonds in a cluster shape, were designed by Garrard in 1863 for the Prince of Wales to give to his bride, Princess Alexandra of Denmark, as part of his wedding gift (page 92). The design had been a popular one since the early 1850s.* ABOVE, LEFT: *Queen Alexandra wearing them at her Coronation on 9 August 1902.* ABOVE, RIGHT: *Queen Mary arriving at the ballet in 1950.* OPPOSITE: *The Queen inherited them from Queen Mary in 1953. Since Queen Elizabeth the Queen Mother has continued to wear the similar trefoil earrings that match the Golden Jubilee necklace, the Queen wears the cluster earrings with it instead.*

QUEEN MARY'S BUTTON EARRINGS

In 1893 a fund was opened by Lady Elizabeth Biddulph to raise money for a wedding present for Princess May of Teck. A pearl and diamond necklace, which could be converted into a tiara, was designed and made by the jewellers Hunt and Roskell (page 15). The presentation was made on behalf of 650 'Ladies of England', and a subsidiary committee, chaired by Lady Clinton, had raised enough money from the 'Ladies of Devonshire' to add a matching pair of pearl button earrings, each with a small diamond on top. In her thank-you letter to Lady Elizabeth, Princess May wrote:

'I shall always value their presents as a token of affection for me and mine, and ever remember their great kindness.'

ABOVE: *Queen Mary, wearing the Devon earrings, at her desk in Buckingham Palace in 1922. She gave the earrings to the Queen in 1947 as a wedding present.* OPPOSITE, ABOVE RIGHT: *The Queen in 1965 at the Presentation of Colours to the 1st Battalion Welsh Guards, of which she is Colonel-in-Chief. Her diamond and platinum brooch is the Regiment's emblem.* OPPOSITE, ABOVE LEFT: *Queen Mary also had a larger pair of earrings in the same style. She wears them here in 1939.* OPPOSITE, BELOW: *The Queen inherited them in 1953. In 1968 she wore them to the Royal Air Force Club. On her left wrist is the diamond and platinum Cartier watch with the smallest face in the world, 5/16 inch in diameter, given to her by the President of the French Republic on her State visit to France in 1957. On her right wrist is a bracelet of diamond links and circles, set with alternate large black and natural pearls.*

Queen Mary's Cluster Earrings and The King George VI and Queen Elizabeth Bandeau Necklace

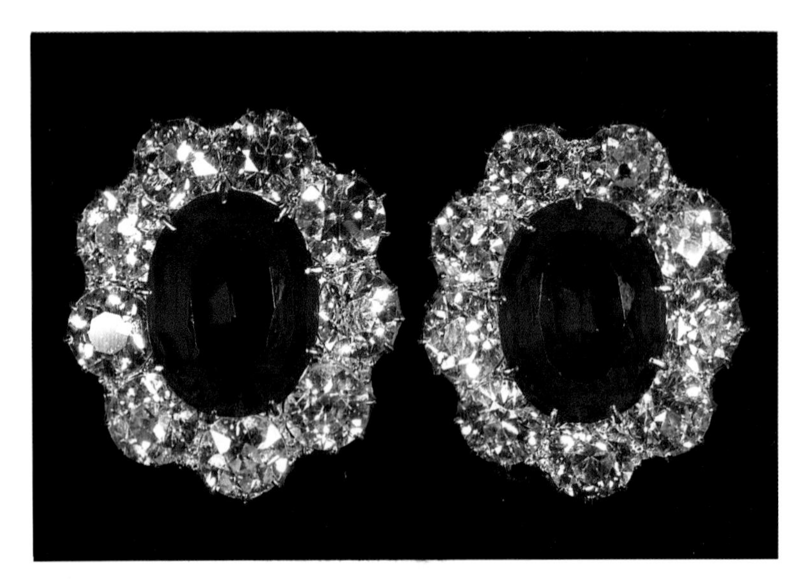

ABOVE, LEFT: *For her fifty-ninth birthday, on 26 May 1926, King George V presented Queen Mary with these earrings – large oval rubies each set in a cluster of nine brilliant-cut diamonds. Later that year, the Queen officially added them to the other pieces of ruby jewellery left to the Crown by Queen Victoria and King Edward VII. Many of these pieces are presently worn by Queen Elizabeth the Queen Mother. Queen Mary's earrings were given to the Queen by her parents in 1947.* ABOVE: *This V-shaped diamond and ruby floral bandeau collar ending in a drop diamond pendant is of Victorian workmanship and was bought by the Queen's parents as a wedding gift.* LEFT: *The Queen arriving at Claridges for a State banquet given by the Greek royal family in 1963. Her wide Art Deco diamond bracelet is formed of eight oblong plaques studded with small rubies.*

Queen Victoria's Fringe Earrings and The Godman Necklace

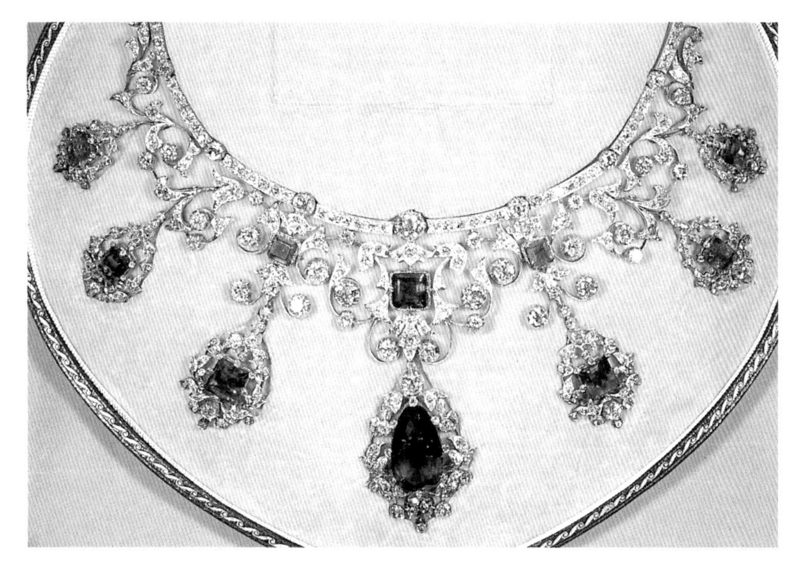

LEFT: *In April of 1850, Queen Victoria purchased a pair of diamond earrings whose emerald drops were framed by a swinging diamond fringe. In her will she left them to the Crown. For King Edward VII's Coronation, on 9 August 1902, Queen Alexandra literally covered her Medici collar and dress of embroidered Indian net with jewels. From her diamond fringe girdle she hung a hem-length double chain, which was caught up in swags by an assortment of brooches. From the bottom two of Queen Victoria's three bow brooches she suspended the emerald fringe earrings as pendants. Her new four-arched crown was made of platinum instead of the traditional gold. Entirely covered with brilliants, the 106-carat Koh-I-Noor diamond is set in the front cross pattée. This is the first occasion on which it was worn at a Coronation, but it is now a tradition that the stone is set in the Queen Consort's crown. The crown is on display in the Jewel House at the Tower of London.* RIGHT: *In 1969 the Queen wore the earrings and the Godman diamond and emerald necklace to a reception at the Schönbrunn Palace in Vienna.* CENTRE: *The Godman necklace, which was thought to have a royal provenance, had been bought by Frederick DuCann Godman, the noted naturalist, expert on the zoology of Central America and a British Museum Trustee, while on holiday in Bavaria in the 1890s. He gave it to his two daughters, and in 1965, long after his death, the elderly spinster sisters wrote to the Lord Chamberlain saying that they believed they owned a piece of jewellery that had once belonged to the Empress Joséphine of France and that this might be of interest to Her Majesty. Sir Francis Watson, Surveyor of the Queen's Works of Art, met them at their bank and inspected the necklace, where it was stored in a vault. Disappointingly, it didn't match the detailed description of an emerald necklace in the inventory of the Empress's jewels, and further investigation in Bavaria, where her son by her first marriage, Eugène de Beauharnais, who married the Princess Amalie Auguste of Bavaria, had retired in 1814 after the overthrow of his stepfather, the Emperor Napoleon, proved that he had never inherited it from his mother. Despite the lack of a royal connection, the Misses Godman said that they would like to present the necklace to the Queen, only requesting that she wear it occasionally. Although it is very rare for a member of the royal family to accept a personal gift from someone they do not know, this was felt to be a special occasion and the Queen, greatly touched by such a generous gesture, was delighted to add the necklace to her collection. Now came the question of how to say thank you; the Godmans might be uncomfortable at a grand lunch or dinner, a large reception or garden party would be too impersonal, and so they were invited to meet the Queen at Buckingham Palace for a private audience.*

Queen Victoria's Golden Jubilee Necklace and Queen Mary's Pendant Earrings

OPPOSITE, BELOW: *In 1887 the 'Women of the British Empire' each gave between a penny and a pound to provide a celebratory memorial for the Queen's fifty years on the throne. Part of the money raised was used to commission a large equestrian statue of Prince Albert, the Prince Consort (not for the Albert Memorial in London, which has often been said erroneously), which the Queen unveiled on Smith's Lawn, Windsor, on 12 May 1890, and the remainder was spent on this necklace, which was presented to Queen Victoria on 24 June 1887. The design is of graduated diamond trefoils, each with a pearl centre. The centrepiece is a quatrefoil of diamonds with a pearl centre and drop pendant. Surmounting it is a pearl and diamond crown. It is possible to detach the centrepiece and wear it as a brooch, which Queen Mary did in the 1920s. Queen Victoria left the necklace to the Crown in 1901. It is interesting that there are at least three necklaces of this design in existence. Princess Alexandra, the Hon. Lady Ogilvy, was given one as a wedding gift by her husband in April 1963, and it only lacks a crown on top of the quatrefoil to be indistinguishable from the Queen's.* OPPOSITE, ABOVE LEFT: *Queen Victoria's official Diamond Jubilee photograph in 1897. She is wearing the necklace as well as the matching diamond trefoil and pearl earrings, which have been worn by Queen Elizabeth the Queen Mother since 1937. The Queen Mother also has the round pearl and diamond cluster brooch.* OPPOSITE, ABOVE CENTRE: *These earrings were converted by Queen Mary from a pendant necklace. Each has an oval pearl suspended from a collet diamond hanging in an ornate frame of scroll design, set with diamonds.* OPPOSITE, ABOVE RIGHT: *Queen Mary, then the Princess of Wales, in about 1902, wearing the pendants on a narrow chain.* ABOVE: *The Queen in Nepal on a State visit in 1986.*

Queen Alexandra's Dagmar Necklace

OPPOSITE, BELOW: *In 1863 Princess Alexandra of Schleswig-Holstein-Sonderburg-Glücksburg's father was the elected heir to the childless King Frederick VII of Denmark. For her marriage to the Prince of Wales that same year, the King had the crown jeweller in Copenhagen, Jules Didrichsen, design a necklace in the Byzantine style. It had 118 pearls and 2,000 diamonds. Festoons connecting gold medallions, with a large diamond in the middle of each, surround a centrepiece of diamond-set scrollwork. The two large pear-shaped pendant pearls on either side were so valuable they had been exhibited at the Great Exhibition at the Crystal Palace in 1851. This is its original case. Hanging on a gold loop from the centrepiece is a cloisonné enamel facsimile of the eleventh-century gold Dagmar Cross, in which was set a fragment reputed to belong to the True Cross and a piece of silk taken from the grave of King Canute. Queen Dagmar had been the benevolent and much loved wife of King Waldemar the Victorious. When she died in 1212, she was buried with this pectoral cross upon her breast, and when her tomb was opened centuries later the cross was removed as a precious relic and put on display in the Museum of Northern Antiquities in Copenhagen. It became a tradition that Danish princesses were given a copy of the cross when they married. The central figure is the head of Christ, with St Basil, St John Chrysostom, St Mary and St John on the four arms.* OPPOSITE, ABOVE LEFT: *Queen Alexandra, when Princess of Wales, wearing the Dagmar Cross hung on a string of pearls.* OPPOSITE, ABOVE RIGHT: *Queen Alexandra at her Coronation on 9 August 1902. She has pinned the Dagmar necklace across her bodice and it can just be seen under the swags of pearls. Queen Victoria's enormous diamond stomacher pinned above it divides into three sections. Queen Mary also wore it at her Coronation in 1911 (page 45), but as an arc; Queen Elizabeth the Queen Mother wore only the centre portion for her Coronation in 1937. Queen Alexandra's diamond fringe girdle had belonged to Queen Victoria, who wore it as a bordure framing the neckline of her dress (page 45).* ABOVE: *The Queen attending a dinner at the German Embassy in London in 1958. She has removed the cross and the two large pearl drops from the Dagmar necklace.*

Queen Victoria's Collet Necklace and Earrings

ABOVE: *Queen Victoria left her collet necklace and earrings to the Crown in 1901. They were made in 1858 from twenty-eight collet stones that she had had removed from a Garter Badge and a ceremonial sword; she wore them when Winterhalter painted her portrait in 1859. The necklace added up to 161 carats, the nine largest stones weighing between 8.25 and 11.25 carats each. The pendant stone, known as the Lahore diamond, and the drops in the earrings come from the Timur ruby necklace, taken from the Treasury of Lahore and presented to Queen Victoria by the Honourable East India Company in 1851.* OPPOSITE, ABOVE LEFT: *This was Queen Victoria's official 1897 Diamond Jubilee Portrait, although the photograph had actually been taken in 1893. Her wide diamond bracelet is now worn by Queen Elizabeth the Queen Mother.* OPPOSITE, ABOVE RIGHT: *Queen Mary wore Queen Victoria's necklace as the bottom row of her diamond collar for her Coronation in 1911, and she wore Queen Victoria's stud earrings instead of the collet drops. The diamond stomacher on her bodice originally belonged to Queen Victoria. Queen Elizabeth the Queen Mother wore just the centre portion at her Coronation in 1937. Queen Mary's crown was made for her and is set only with diamonds, including the*

106-carat Koh-I-Noor, which can be seen in the front. In 1937 Queen Elizabeth removed the detachable Lahore pendant from the collet necklace, had it cut down to 22.48 carats and wore it inserted in her new crown for the Coronation, wearing the necklace as a plain collet chain. At the same time she took out two of the large stones, replacing them with three smaller ones from another Crown collet necklace, and made another pair of earrings. Today there are twenty-nine collets and the three pendants from the Timur ruby necklace in the set of necklace and earrings. ABOVE, LEFT: *Queen Elizabeth photographed in 1939. Her second chain of forty-five collets was also left to the Crown by Queen Victoria.* ABOVE, RIGHT: *The Queen wore the necklace and earrings at her Coronation in 1953, and here, in 1961, at a formal ceremony on an official visit to Sierra Leone.*

The King Faisal of Saudi Arabia Necklace

The King Khalid of Saudi Arabia Necklace

OPPOSITE, ABOVE: *King Faisal of Saudi Arabia bought this fringe necklace of drop diamonds set with brilliants and baguettes made by the American jeweller Harry Winston and presented it to the Queen in 1967 on a State visit to England. The Queen wore it on the last night of his visit when he gave a banquet at the Dorchester Hotel in her honour.* OPPOSITE, RIGHT: *In 1979 the Queen wore the necklace to a film premiere together with a pair of antique diamond girandole earrings, a triple-pendant design that Queen Victoria had been very partial to more than a hundred years earlier.* OPPOSITE, LEFT: *In 1983 the Queen loaned the necklace to the Princess of Wales for her visit to Australia.*
ABOVE, LEFT: *Another gift from Saudi Arabia, this modern collar of round and pear-shaped diamonds in a sunray design made by Harry Winston, was given to the Queen by King Khalid when she made a State visit to his country in February 1979. She wears it here to a film premiere in 1982.* ABOVE, RIGHT: *She loaned it to the Princess of Wales to wear on at least three occasions during 1982 and 1983. Here the Princess wears it with a pair of ornate diamond and pearl drop earrings, which were given to her as a wedding present by the Amir of Qatar.*

The Cambridge and Delhi Durbar Parure

This, the most magnificent parure of jewellery in the Queen's possession, was created by Queen Mary, using stones from four different sources, and endures as a tribute to her taste and majestic sense of style. The story begins in 1818, when King George III's seventh and favourite son, Adolphus, Duke of Cambridge, married Princess Augusta of Hesse, who was twenty-one to his forty-four. While they were visiting Frankfurt, a State lottery was held in aid of charity; the Duchess bought some tickets and won a small box containing some forty graduated cabochon emeralds. Back in England she used some of them to make a pair of drop earrings and a necklace with five pendant stones.

RIGHT: *At her death in 1889 at York House, St James's Palace, the earrings, necklace and remaining emeralds became the property of her younger daughter, Princess Mary Adelaide, Duchess of Teck. She is photographed wearing the earrings and necklace around 1893. The Duchess had previously bought her diamond stomacher from Garrard, and set another of the emeralds in it, 'surrounding the emerald with two rows of diamonds. A second emerald was set in a diamond leaf mount and hung as a pendant from the bottom of the stomacher. When the Duchess died intestate in 1897, her jewellery was divided among her four children. Her daughter, Queen Mary, then the Duchess of York and living in her grandmother's old home, York House, took this striking diamond tiara with its design of crescents and stars, and large diamond necklace of interconnecting circles. The Duchess of Teck had worn both of these*

pieces at her daughter's wedding in 1893 at the Chapel Royal, St James's Palace. In the 1930s Queen Mary gave the tiara to her daughter-in-law Queen Elizabeth, after removing the bottom two rows of diamonds so that it sat much lower on the head; she also gave the diamond necklace to Queen Elizabeth, who later passed it on to Princess Margaret.

The Duchess of Teck's second son, the unmarried Prince Francis, got the emeralds, including the centrepiece and pendant from the stomacher, which itself went to the youngest son, Prince Alexander. When Prince Alexander married Princess Alice of Albany, Queen Victoria's granddaughter, in 1904, he had new detachable centre brooches set with sapphires he had inherited from his mother made for the stomacher and gave it to his bride. As Princess Alice, the Countess of Athlone, she remembered, in old age, wearing it at three Coronations: King George V's, King George VI's and the Queen's. On 28 June 1910, Queen Mary was given the cleavings from the Cullinan by the Union of South Africa: six large stones and ninety-six small brilliants. Less than six months later, on 22 October, her brother Francis died suddenly at the age of forty. He had given his mother's emeralds to his mistress, but within days of his funeral Queen Mary bravely sent an emissary to the lady asking her to return the jewels, which she did. Now the Queen had the Cambridge emeralds and the 102 Cullinan cleavings with which to make a completely new set of jewellery as she prepared for her Coronation, on 22 June 1911, and the Delhi Durbar, on 12 December, when she would be acclaimed Empress of India. The Indian word 'durbar' means both a gathering of chieftains to make administrative decisions and a purely ceremonial gathering at which they paid homage to their ruler.

Queen Mary had a new diamond crown made for the Coronation, but an Act of Parliament dating from the time of King Edward III, who tried to pawn the Crown Jewels in Flanders to finance a war with France, prevents the Regalia from being taken out of the United Kingdom, and so King George V had commissioned an Indian Crown especially for the Delhi ceremony. Even though Queen Mary's crown was her personal property she decided not to take it either, but to design a new diadem for the occasion. While the jewellers were working on her new parure, Queen Mary was informed that the 'Ladies of India' wished to make her a gift of jewellery to mark the occasion of the Durbar. She suggested that the gift should be Indian emeralds to add to the new set and so a second necklace and a brooch were made to co-ordinate with the other pieces. In June 1911, the Queen wore her mother's original necklace, the Cambridge emerald earrings and brooch made from the two emerald parts of the stomacher (page 49, above), for her son David's Investiture as Prince of Wales at Carnarvon Castle, but she was photographed in the new parure later that month.

PAGE 49: *Queen Mary photographed in 1912 after returning from India, wearing the complete parure. Her new high scroll-and-festoon diamond tiara surmounted by five of the Cambridge emeralds was described by King George V in a letter about the Durbar to his mother, Queen Alexandra, as 'May's best tiara'. The emerald and diamond cluster earrings matched the diamond chain bracelet with its three cluster plaques on her right wrist. The delicate emerald choker with its connecting rosettes of small brilliants was also made from the Cambridge stones; but the larger necklace and negligé pendant below it was the gift from the 'Ladies of India', as was the ancient engraved square emerald brooch pinned on the right of her bodice. In Delhi, on 9 December, the Queen received the Maharani of Patiala and some of the ladies from her committee, who ceremoniously presented her with the necklace and brooch she had planned so carefully back in London. In her personally written thank-you speech she said:*

'The jewel you have given me will ever be very precious in my eyes, and, whenever I wear it, though thousands of miles of land and sea separate us, my thoughts will fly to the homes of India, and create again and again this happy meeting and recall the tender love

your hearts have yielded me. Your jewel shall pass to future generations as an imperial heirloom, and shall always stand as a token of the first meeting of an English Queen with the ladies of India.'

Three days later, dressed in her heavily embroidered Coronation gown, she wore the complete parure at the Durbar. When Queen Mary sent photographs of the splendid occasion to her aunt, the Grand Duchess of Mecklenburg-Strelitz, she wrote back:

'Mama's Emeralds appearing there *amused and pleased me. What would she have said to her Grandchild's Imperial glory? in which I so rejoice!'*

PAGE 48, ABOVE: *The Cambridge earrings, oval cabochon emeralds, each set in a cluster of eleven brilliant-cut diamonds.* PAGE 48, BELOW: *The 'Ladies of India' necklace has eight cabochon emeralds surrounded by diamonds, set in two chains of small diamonds, with a single large diamond between each emerald. Typically Edwardian was the removable negligé pendant of two drops of unequal length; the large pear-shaped emerald was part of the Indian gift, but the 11.5-carat marquise-cut diamond was the Cullinan VI, which King Edward had bought from Asscher in 1908 and given to Queen Alexandra as a gift. After his death she gave it to Queen Mary, who added it to the necklace. For certain ceremonial occasions, such as the Opening of Parliament in 1913, however, she suspended the 94.4-carat Cullinan III diamond as the pendant drop instead.* OPPOSITE: *In 1921 Queen Mary bought from Princess Nicholas of Greece the diamond and pearl tiara she had inherited on the death of her mother, the Grand Duchess Vladimir of Russia (page 24). Over the following years the refugee Princess Nicholas sold a number of pieces of jewellery in order to help support her family and worthy Russian charities. The Queen still had fifteen of the Cambridge cabochon emeralds left, and these were now put in pavé-set diamond mounts, and the tiara adapted so that it could be worn with either the pearl or the emerald drops.* ABOVE: *Queen Mary wearing the tiara in 1937, together with the 'Ladies of India' necklace from which she had removed the negligé pendant. The 'Ladies of India' carved emerald brooch pinned to her Garter sash was left to the Queen, but she has never worn it.* LEFT: *The Queen inherited the parure on her grandmother's death in 1953 and wears it here in 1957.*

OPPOSITE, ABOVE LEFT: *The stomacher of Cambridge emeralds and small Cullinan chips, which was designed in 1911, comes apart, so that it can be worn as separate brooches. In the centre is the 18.8-carat heart-shaped Cullinan V (page 86). From the 6.8-carat oblong Cullinan VIII hangs an emerald drop (page 87).* OPPOSITE, ABOVE CENTRE: *The cabochon emerald brooch surrounded by two circles of diamonds and with an emerald drop, pinned at the bottom of the stomacher, was made by simply putting together the two Victorian pieces removed from the Duchess of Teck's stomacher in 1897 (page 49).* OPPOSITE, ABOVE RIGHT: *Queen Mary wearing the brooch in 1925. Following her brother Francis's death in 1910, she wore it at the Prince of Wales's Investiture in June 1911.* OPPOSITE, BELOW LEFT: *One of the Queen's favourite brooches, she wears it here in 1979.* OPPOSITE, BELOW CENTRE: *This diamond scroll brooch with a central lozenge-shaped emerald was made by taking the main portion from the centre of the stomacher and hanging the emerald drop from Cullinan VIII from it. It is possible to see where the two parts are connected.* OPPOSITE, BELOW RIGHT: *The Queen arriving for the 1967 Derby. She is also wearing a unique pair of pearl button earrings that have a small diamond on both the top and bottom.* LEFT: *By 1927, Queen Mary had had the delicate choker of Cambridge emeralds, made in 1911, redesigned in the fashionable Art Deco style. The diamond-encircled cabochon stones are now divided by geometric diamond plaques, each with a small emerald centre. The bangle bracelet set with two oval emeralds on her right wrist was part of the original parure. The Art Deco choker was left to the Queen, but she has never worn it. In 1981 she took it out of storage and gave it to the Princess of Wales as a wedding gift. That December, the Princess had the fourteen-inch-long necklace mounted on a band of dark green Velcro, so that she could wear it as a headband at a private party during the Christmas holidays.* RIGHT: *Instead of a tiara, she wore the necklace across her forehead as a bandeau, for the first time in public, at a charity dance on her visit to Australia in 1984. Her long pendant diamond earrings with an oval emerald drop, and a diamond Art Deco bracelet with zigzag bands of emeralds (not seen here), were bought by Prince Charles as a wedding gift at Wartski Ltd in 1981.*

Queen Alexandra's Indian Necklace

ABOVE, CENTRE: *In 1863, one of Princess Alexandra of Denmark's wedding gifts from Queen Victoria was a suite of Indian ornaments, comprising a collar, armlet and two bracelets, made from uncut emeralds, diamonds and pearls. The seven-row collar of pearl and emerald beads was hung with a multitude of diamond pendants with emerald or pearl drops.* ABOVE, LEFT: *Queen Alexandra, then Princess of Wales, on 2 July 1897, at the Duchess of Devonshire's costume ball to celebrate Queen Victoria's Diamond Jubilee. The Indian necklace lies just below her dog-collar.* BELOW, LEFT: *In the 1920s Queen Mary broke up the piece. She made a rope of the pearl and emerald beads, which she wore before giving them to her daughter-in-law, Princess Alice, Duchess of Gloucester, as a wedding gift in 1935, and she gave one of the diamond pendants, with a pearl drop, on a thin gold chain to her first granddaughter, Princess Elizabeth, who wears it here in 1931 for her official fifth-birthday photograph.* RIGHT: *In 1960 ten-year-old Princess Anne was photographed with her month-old baby brother, Prince Andrew, wearing her mother's necklace.* ABOVE, RIGHT: *An identical necklace was given to the Queen's niece, Lady Sarah Armstrong-Jones, who is photographed with her mother, Princess Margaret, and her brother, Viscount Linley.*

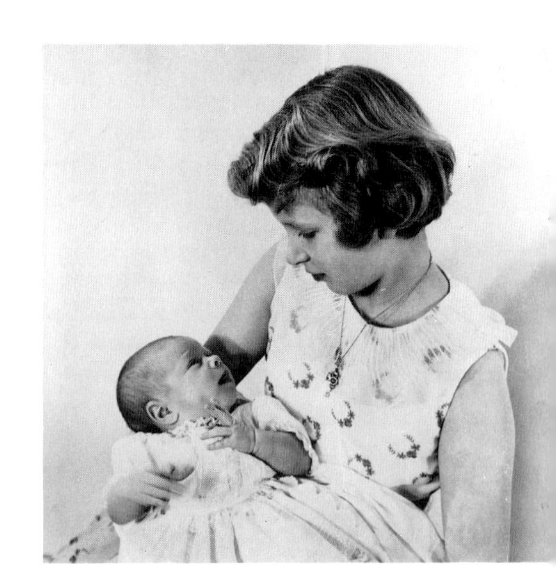

THE QUEEN'S FIRST NECKLACE

As a nine-month-old baby in December 1926, Princess Elizabeth's jewellery collection was started in the same unostentatious manner as that of any other daughter of the aristocracy. Not for the royal family a gaudy display of nouveau-riche wealth with strings of diamonds or sparkling clips from fashionable Bond Street jewellers. Instead, the first-born child of the young Duke and Duchess of York was given a delicate string of her mother's own childhood pink coral beads just before her parents had to leave her behind for six months while they represented King George V on a goodwill tour of Australia and New Zealand.
After they sailed in HMS Renown, *the baby Princess often stayed with her grandparents, and Queen Mary, knowing how painful it was for her son and daughter-in-law to miss their daughter's first tooth, step and words, had photographs taken of her every month and sent out to them. The Princess wore her coral necklace for these and in most of her childhood pictures until 1940.* ABOVE: *Queen Elizabeth the Queen Mother, aged two, in August 1902, wearing her coral bead necklace.* ABOVE, RIGHT: *The Queen in 1927. Pearls have been added to the coral beads, and she plays with an ivory-handled rattle given her by Queen Mary.* RIGHT: *Princess Anne photographed with her mother to mark her first birthday in 1951. She is not only wearing the same necklace and playing with the same rattle, but the picture was taken by the same photographer, Marcus Adams.*

THE QUEEN'S FIRST PEARL NECKLACE

Queen Victoria started a family tradition by giving each of her five daughters two fine pearls a year from birth, so that when they were grown-up they would have enough for a necklace. However, by 1866, when she was also buying pearls for a growing number of granddaughters, Queen Victoria asked her eldest daughter, Vicky, married to the Prussian Crown Prince, to explain to her sisters that with the price of a pearl having risen to between £30 and £40 she had to cut back and could only provide one a year for their daughters, since she was still making up the necklaces of her own two youngest daughters, Louise and Beatrice.

BELOW: *King George VI followed his great-grandmother's example and gave the Queen a thin platinum chain to which he added two pearls on each birthday. She wears it here, aged three, in 1929.*

RIGHT: *Princess Anne wore the necklace at her mother's Coronation, and here in 1954, when she was four years old. The Queen's diamond and drop-pearl earrings were a wedding present from the Sheikh of Bahrain. Her two rows of large pearls, which fasten with an oval diamond-cluster clasp, had originally been part of the Hanoverian collection. They are Crown property and passed to the Queen when Queen Mary died in 1953. The Queen wore the necklace at Prince Andrew's wedding in 1986, with the clasp showing on the side, and no brooch, a nearly unprecedented break in her personal style.*

Her brooch in this picture is the one she had designed by Frederick A. Mew of Cartier as a setting for the 54.5-carat rare pink diamond she had been given by John T. Williamson as a wedding gift in 1947. Dr Williamson was an eccentric Canadian, who had discovered a diamond mine in Mwadui, Tanganyika, in 1940, when he was only thirty-three. He developed it into the richest diamond-bearing mine in the world, giving him an annual income of £2,000,000. In October 1947, the year he sold out to De Beers, the mine yielded the finest pink diamond ever seen, and Dr Williamson, a fanatical monarchist, sent it to Princess Elizabeth. In March 1948, accompanied by Queen Mary, the Princess went to the Clerkenwell factory of Briefel & Lemer, in East London, to watch the diamond being cut into a 23.6-carat brilliant. Dr Williamson supplied a number of small white diamonds to be used in the platinum setting, but because he had hoped to find more pink diamonds to add to his original gift, work on the brooch was postponed until 1952. Then the 'Williamson Pink' became the centre of a jonquil-shaped flower with curved petals of navette-cut diamonds, a stem of baguette diamonds and two large navette-cut diamonds as leaves. The brooch is 4½ inches long.

The King George V Jubilee Necklace

ABOVE: *When King George V celebrated his Silver Jubilee, on 6 May 1935, he gave his two granddaughters their first serious jewellery: pearl necklaces. Princess Elizabeth was given three perfectly matched rows, and Princess Margaret, being four years younger, two rows. The Princesses, who wore their pearls for their parents' Coronation two years later, are seen here with them in 1938.*

The Queen Anne and The Queen Caroline Necklaces

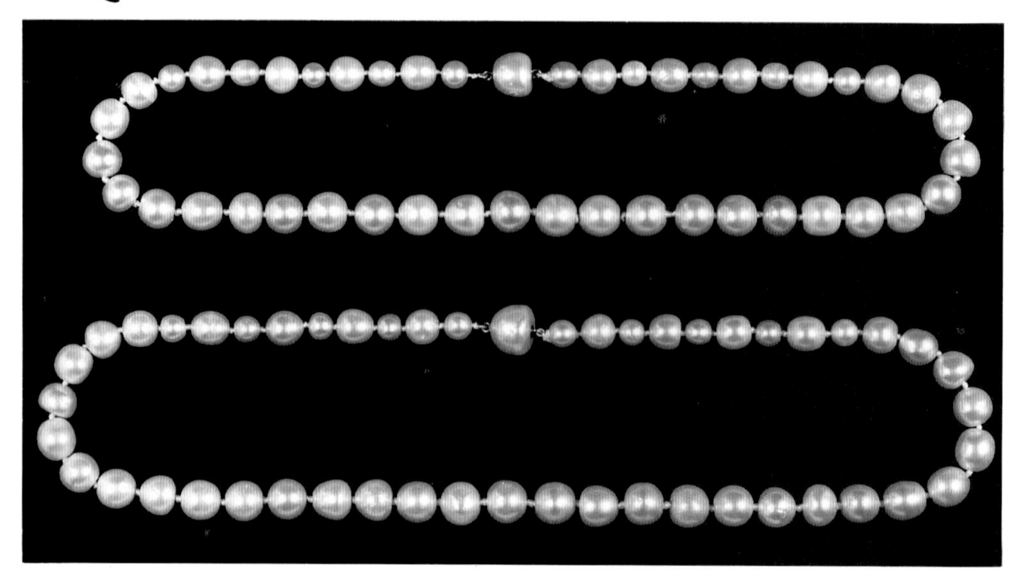

ABOVE: *These two rows of large, lustrous, graduated pearls, with pearl clasps, are always worn together and were left to the Crown by Queen Victoria. The top row, of forty-six pearls, weighs 1,045 grammes and is said to have belonged to Queen Anne, the last of the Stuart monarchs. Horace Walpole wrote in his diary:*

'Queen Anne had but few jewels and those indifferent, except one pearl necklace given her by Prince George.'

Queen Caroline, the wife of King George II, had a great deal of valuable jewellery, including four very fine pearl necklaces. After wearing all of them at her Coronation, the fifty best pearls were made into a single necklace – the bottom row of the pair – which weighs 1,429.2 grammes. In 1947 both necklaces were given to Princess Elizabeth as a wedding present by her father King George VI. BELOW: *Princess Elizabeth was married to Prince Philip on 20 November 1947. John Colville had recently been appointed her Private Secretary, and was to travel to Westminster Abbey in her carriage procession. Half an hour before they were scheduled to leave Buckingham Palace he was summoned to her second-floor sitting room. The two-row pearl necklace her father had given her had been left on display with all the other wedding gifts at St James's Palace and she particularly wanted to wear them. Could Colville get to St James's and bring them back? He rushed down the seemingly endless red-carpeted corridor, hurtled down the Grand Staircase, and ended up in the quadrangle, where he commandeered King Haakon VII of Norway's large Daimler. Although traffic had been stopped since early morning,*

THE QUEEN'S FOUR ROW CHOKER

the crowds were so deeply packed across Marlborough Gate, that the car, even flying its royal flag, had to halt while he fought his way through on foot. When he arrived at the Friary Court entrance to the State Apartments there was only an elderly janitor to listen to his odd story, but he finally allowed Colville upstairs to explain his mission to the CID men who were guarding the 2,660 presents. Their dilemma was: if they accepted his story and he turned out to be a clever jewel thief who had made off with the Crown pearls, they were in trouble; but if they refused to let him have the necklace and it all turned out to be true, they were equally in trouble. There was no one to consult; time was running out, and only after they had found his name in the wedding programme as one of the Household officials in attendance on the Princess did they allow him to remove the pearls. This portrait was taken in the Music Room of Buckingham Palace after the ceremony.

RIGHT: *The Queen had this four-row choker made from pearls in her collection. The large, conical, diamond-studded clasp is deep enough for her to add another two rows of pearls, if she desires.* LEFT: *In 1982 the Queen loaned the necklace to the Princess of Wales to wear at a banquet at Hampton Court Palace, given by Queen Beatrix and Prince Claus of the Netherlands, who were in England on a State visit.*

LEFT: *The Empress Marie Feodorovna, Queen Alexandra's younger sister, had one of the world's most valuable collections of jewellery, but her favourite jewels were her pearls. Interspersed in this four-row choker of 164 pearls are twenty diamond-studded vertical bars, between every two pearls at the front, and between every three pearls at the back. The necklace is made to convert into two bracelets, and the octagonal clasp is a large sapphire surrounded by two rows of diamonds. Following her death in exile in Denmark in 1928, after the Russian Revolution, her jewels were sold in England by Hennell and Sons.* RIGHT: *Queen Mary bought the necklace as well as a number of other pieces of jewellery, and she wore it here in 1931. Her small V-shaped tiara with a large centre sapphire had also belonged to the Empress. Queen Mary left the tiara to Queen Elizabeth the Queen Mother, who has never worn it in public, but loaned it to Princess Margaret for a number of years.* BELOW, LEFT: *The Queen inherited the necklace in 1953. She wore it with the clasp in front at the Horse of the Year Show in 1956.* BELOW, RIGHT: *In 1960 she wore it to an Order of the British Empire Service at St Paul's Cathedral, turned around with the clasp at the back.* OPPOSITE: *The Queen has loaned the necklace to Princess Anne, and she wears it here in 1974 on a visit to Toronto. Her diamond tiara was presented to her by the World Wide Shipping Group after she launched their tanker* World Unicorn *in 1973.*

THE EMPRESS MARIE FEODOROVNA OF RUSSIA'S NECKLACE

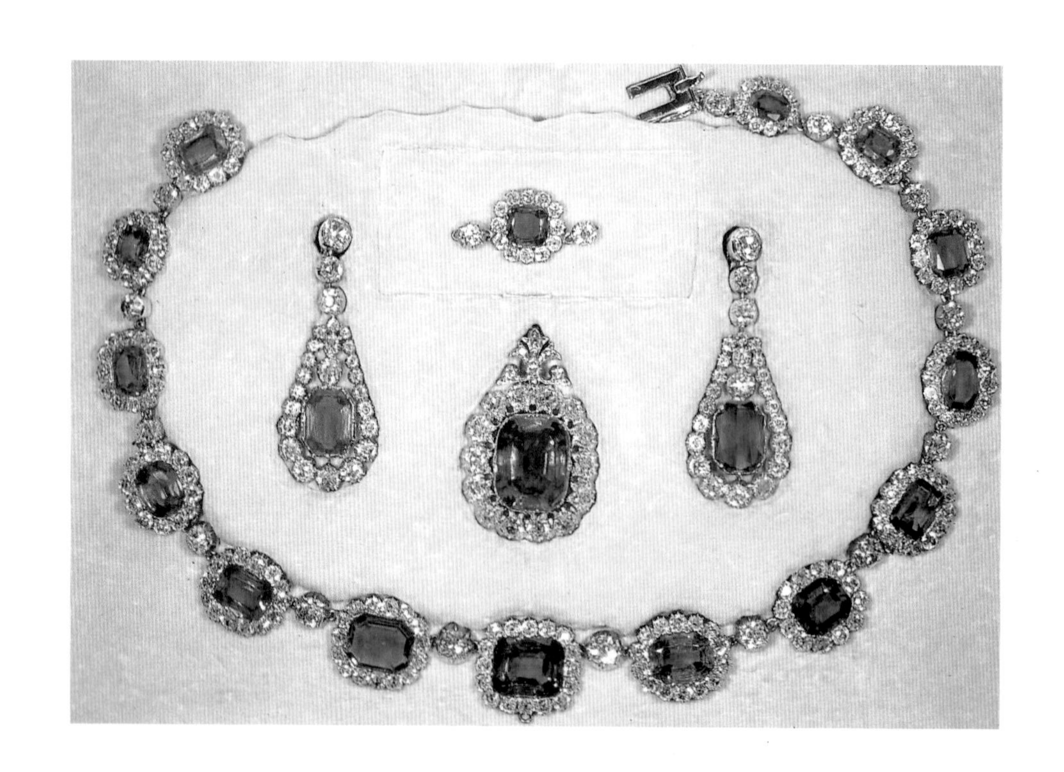

The King George VI Victorian Suite

In 1947 King George gave Princess Elizabeth a long necklace of oblong sapphires surrounded by round diamonds and separated by diamond collets as a wedding gift. To match it there was a pair of free-swinging, square-shaped sapphire earrings, bordered with diamonds and hanging from three collet stones. The suite was made around 1850. The colour of the stones exactly matched the blue of the Garter Riband, although this choice may have been a coincidence on the part of the King. In 1952 the Queen had the necklace shortened by removing the largest stone, plus one of the smaller sapphires, and in 1959 a pendant was made using the big stone.

OPPOSITE, ABOVE: *The King George VI sapphire suite in its velvet case, including the extra link that was removed.* OPPOSITE, BELOW: *Princess Elizabeth photographed in her drawing room at Clarence House before leaving for an official visit to Kenya in 1952. King George VI died while she was there, and this picture was withheld from distribution until after the end of Court mourning on 1 June 1952. The necklace is its original length. When Noel Coward saw her wearing the suite at the 1954 Royal Command Performance at the Palladium, he wrote:*

'After the show we lined up and were presented to the Queen, Prince Philip and Princess Margaret. The Queen looked luminously lovely and was wearing the largest sapphires I have ever seen.'

ABOVE: *In 1963 a new sapphire and diamond tiara and bracelet were made to match the original pieces. The Queen wore the complete parure when she and Prince Philip attended a charity concert in 1969.*

THE PRESIDENT AYUB KHAN OF PAKISTAN NECKLACE

ABOVE: *In 1966 the President of Pakistan, Field-Marshal Mohammed Ayub Khan, made a State visit to Britain and gave the Queen a two-row pearl necklace hung with graduated turquoise pendants ending in seed pearl drops. Her Majesty wears it at a dinner during the visit. When Princess Anne was a teenager the necklace was divided into two. Six small pendants from the lower row were removed and added to the shorter strand so that it now has pendants all the way around. A pair of earrings was made from two rosettes out of the extra centrepiece, with the last two small pendants being suspended as drops.* LEFT: *Princess Anne wore the set to a dinner at the Royal Academy in June 1986.*

The Kent Demi-Parure

The Kent demi-parure is the oldest set of jewellery in the royal collection, and was owned by Queen Victoria's mother, the Duchess of Kent, who, as the widowed Princess of Leiningen, had married King George III's fourth son in 1817. When she died at Frogmore on 16 March 1861, aged seventy-five, she left all her property to the Queen, and Prince Albert was named sole executor of her estate. In the nineteenth century amethysts were very popular and as a result quite valuable, and in her 1901 will Queen Victoria left these jewels to the Crown. The set consisted of a necklace, three brooches, a pair of earrings and a pair of hair combs.

ABOVE, LEFT: *In this engraving after the 1839 miniature by Sir William Ross, the Duchess of Kent wears only the brooch.*

ABOVE, RIGHT: *Queen Elizabeth also wore only the brooch as she, the King and the two Princesses looked over the itinerary for the royal couple's forthcoming visit to the United States and Canada in 1939.*

RIGHT: *The Queen wearing the demi-parure on her State visit to Portugal in 1984. The central pendant with its small diamond drop matches the earrings, and the sunray design of diamonds surrounding the two side stones in the necklace is the same as that around the brooch.*

QUEEN VICTORIA'S BOW BROOCHES

ABOVE: *Bow-knot brooches have been popular since the seventeenth century, and in May of 1858 Garrard made a set of three bow brooches, two large and one small, out of 506 diamonds supplied by Queen Victoria. Although it seems that there is no pictorial record to prove that Queen Victoria ever wore them herself, Queen Alexandra and Queen Mary both wore them at their Coronations.* OPPOSITE, ABOVE LEFT: *Queen Alexandra, in mourning for Queen Victoria at the first State Opening of Parliament of the new reign in 1901, wore the bow brooches on her skirt, and suspended from each one a chain of round diamond clusters, usually joined together as a necklace, with a large oval diamond drop on the end of each. She also wore the small diamond crown covered in 1,300 diamonds that Queen Victoria had had made in 1870, as she found the Imperial State Crown uncomfortably heavy to wear (page 76, top left). The diamond waterfall brooch on her collar and the wide diamond bracelet were both worn by Queen Victoria and are owned by Queen Elizabeth the Queen Mother at present.* OPPOSITE, ABOVE CENTRE: *For this formal photograph in 1912, Queen Mary wore all three of the bow brooches. From the top one is suspended the pear-shaped Cullinan III diamond and from the bottom two bows she has hung two large oval diamond drops. Directly above the bows is the 106-carat Koh-I-Noor diamond in a brooch setting.* OPPOSITE, ABOVE RIGHT: *Queen Elizabeth the Queen Mother wore just one bow in 1938, along with her signature rows of large lustrous pearls, although she sometimes wore the two big brooches as a set.* OPPOSITE, BELOW LEFT: *The Queen only ever wears one, as here in 1971.* OPPOSITE, BELOW RIGHT: *It is a tradition that members of the royal family who are staying at Balmoral for their summer*

holidays attend the annual Braemar Highland Games. In September 1986, just two months after her marriage to Prince Andrew, the Duchess of York came to the Games for the first time, where she is pictured here with Prince Charles. Pinned at the collar of her white blouse is one of the bows, a loan from the Queen. Her traditional pearl and diamond button earrings were a wedding gift.

Queen Mary's Kensington Bow Brooch and Surrey Brooch

ABOVE: *In July 1893, the committee of the Kensington Wedding-Gift Fund, representing the inhabitants of Kensington, visited Princess May of Teck's home at White Lodge, Richmond, to present her with this bow-shaped diamond brooch with a large oriental pearl drop. It was made by Collingwood and Company. She wore the brooch at King Edward VII's Coronation in 1902, and at her own in 1911, as an appropriate symbol of her childhood at Kensington Palace.* LEFT: *A line drawing of the brooch given to Princess May as a wedding present by the Ladies of Surrey Needlework Guild.* OPPOSITE, ABOVE LEFT: *The Duke and Duchess of York at the Duchess of Devonshire's Costume Ball on 2 July 1897, to celebrate Queen Victoria's Diamond Jubilee. Dressed in sky-blue satin, the Duchess has attached the Surrey brooch as a pendant to her five-row pearl necklace, which was a wedding gift from her husband. Framing the neckline of her bodice is the pearl and diamond necklace that was a wedding gift from the 'Ladies of England' (page 15). Below that is the Kensington bow brooch, and pinned below the diamond stomacher is the Dorset bow brooch. The enormous baroque pearl brooch pinned at the corner of her bodice originally belonged to Queen Alexandra, and was given to Princess Alice, Duchess of Gloucester, as a wedding gift by Queen Mary in 1935.* OPPOSITE, ABOVE RIGHT: *The Queen inherited the Kensington and Surrey brooches in 1953. She wore the Surrey brooch pinned to her Garter sash to open the New South Wales Parliament, in Sydney, Australia, in 1954, the only time she has worn it in public.* OPPOSITE, BELOW: *She wore the Kensington bow brooch in July 1986 when she attended a dinner given by the President of West Germany during his State visit to Great Britain. Her six-row pearl necklace set with different-sized diamond plaques and the matching earrings were a gift to the Queen from the Amir of Qatar on her 1979 visit to the Gulf States.*

Queen Mary's True Lover's Knot Brooch

Prince Philip's Naval Badge Brooch

OPPOSITE, ABOVE RIGHT: *A large diamond bow in a 'true lover's knot' design with scalloped edges and pendant tassels.* OPPOSITE, LEFT: *Queen Mary painted by Sir Oswald Birley in April 1934. He painted the King at the same time, and when Queen Mary went to inspect the two portraits in the painter's studio on 4 May, she judged them as 'good'. In addition to the lover's knot brooch, she is wearing a diamond choker necklace that she gave to Queen Elizabeth the Queen Mother, who has shortened it into a bracelet.* OPPOSITE, BELOW RIGHT: *The Queen in July 1986 at a State banquet at Buckingham Palace. She inherited the brooch from Queen Mary in 1953. Here she wears with it the new tiara – a wreath of flowers made from Burmese rubies and diamonds – that she commissioned Garrard to make in 1973. The earrings are miniature flowers, the rubies edged with a circle of brilliant- and baguette-cut diamonds. Her nineteenth-century necklace of rubies surrounded by diamonds has a chatelaine centre in a design of currant leaves and clusters of fruit that can be detached and worn as a stomacher or hair ornament. It was sold at Sotheby's by a member of the Baring family in April 1964 and purchased on behalf of Her Majesty. The stones for the tiara and earrings came from the Queen's private collection. She had been given a necklace of ninety-six rubies set in gold by the people of Burma as a wedding gift. The number ninety-six is significant because there is a Burmese tradition that there are ninety-six diseases that can affect the human body, and each of the rubies symbolized a charm against an illness, so that 'the recipient will be as impervious to the ninety-six diseases as is the lotus leaf to water'. The diamonds came from a tiara the Queen had been given as a wedding gift by the Nizam of Hyderabad and Berar* *(page 106, right).*

RIGHT: *Prince Philip was still a serving officer in the Royal Navy at the time of his marriage to Princess Elizabeth in November 1947. One of his first gifts to her was this miniature naval badge brooch set in diamonds. She wears it here in September 1950 as she poses in her sitting room at Clarence House for Princess Anne's first photograph, one month after her birth.*

Queen Mary's Dorset Bow Brooch

Queen Elizabeth the Queen Mother's Maple Leaf Brooch

ABOVE, LEFT: *When the King and Queen visited Canada in 1939, Her Majesty was presented with a large diamond-encrusted maple leaf brooch, the national emblem, which she wore constantly during the war pinned to her shoulder, hat or even on the side of a pochette bag. She wears it here at Royal Lodge, Windsor, in 1940. The gift followed a long tradition: in 1901 Queen Mary, then the Duchess of York, visited Canada as part of a seven-month-long tour of the Empire and she was given an enamel maple leaf spray by the ladies of Montreal. In 1923, Queen Elizabeth, then the Duchess of York, received as a wedding gift from the Canadian Legion of the British Empire Service League a gold maple leaf brooch set with diamonds.* ABOVE, RIGHT: *In 1951 Princess Elizabeth and Prince Philip toured Canada for the first time and the Princess borrowed her mother's brooch to wear during the trip.*

OPPOSITE, ABOVE: *This fancy ribbon-bow brooch set with fine brilliants was made by Carrington and Company and presented as a wedding gift to Queen Mary in 1893 by the 'County of Dorset'.* OPPOSITE, LEFT: *Queen Mary, then the Duchess of York, wearing the brooch in 1898. Her diamond tiara had been a wedding gift from Lord and Lady Iveagh. She left it to Princess Alice, Duchess of Gloucester, who has given it to her daughter-in-law the present Duchess.* OPPOSITE, RIGHT: *Queen Mary gave the brooch to Princess Elizabeth as a wedding present in 1947. She wears it for this formal portrait with Prince Philip in the drawing room of their home, Clarence House, in 1952.*

THE QUEEN'S IVY LEAF BROOCHES

ABOVE: *The royal family were on their official visit to South Africa at the time of Princess Elizabeth's twenty-first birthday on 21 April 1947, but her parents had come prepared with this twin pair of Cartier ivy leaf brooches, each covered with pavé-set diamonds and a large round brilliant in the centre.* RIGHT: *The Queen in 1951 wearing them as lapel brooches; she also wore them on her hat, or to accentuate the corners of a square neckline.*

Queen Victoria's Wheat Ear Brooches

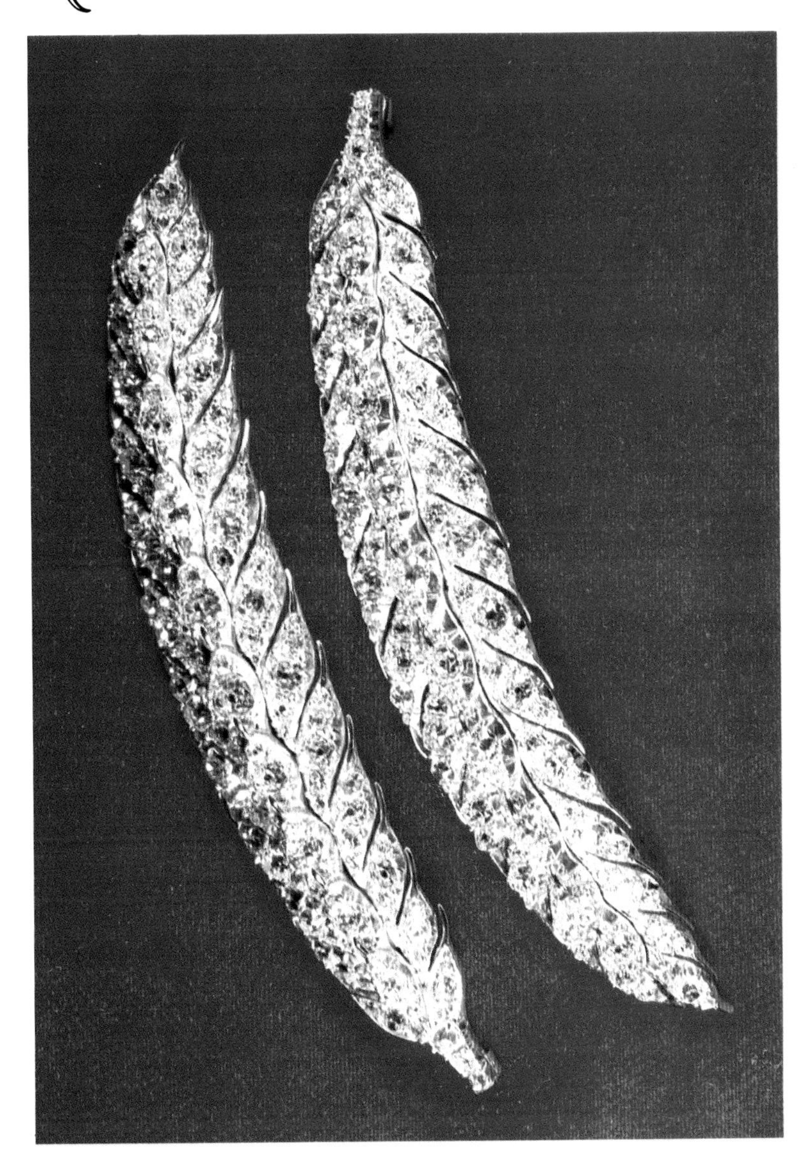

ABOVE: *In 1830 the new King William IV ordered six brooches that could also be worn as hair ornaments. They were made from diamonds that had belonged to his father, King George III, and were replicas of wheat ears, a popular motif of the period. In her will Queen Victoria designated them as Crown jewellery.* ABOVE, RIGHT: *Queen Victoria in an unusual 1896 hand-tinted photograph when she was seventy-seven years old. She is wearing three of the brooches pinned along the curve of her neckline. In addition to her diamond tiara, she has a number of small brooches pinned to the crown of her lace veil.* RIGHT: *The Queen at the Royal Opera House in 1974 wearing two of the ears as hair slides. Other royal ladies such as Princess Anne, the Duchess of York, the Duchess of Kent, the Duchess of Gloucester and Princess Michael of Kent also often enhance an evening hairstyle with sparkling combs and slides.*

Queen Victoria's Bar Brooch

ABOVE: *In 1839 Queen Victoria wore two bar brooches of collet diamonds, pinned about three inches apart, to keep her Garter Riband securely in place (page 99, above left). Later she had them reset as a double bar brooch, which she left to the Crown in her will, its description tucked away in a long list of jewelled Orders.* OPPOSITE, ABOVE LEFT: *Queen Victoria photographed in 1893 as Empress of India.* OPPOSITE, ABOVE RIGHT: *Queen Alexandra photographed in 1913. The beaded net of her dress was woven for her in India and the circlet is the one that Queen Victoria had made in 1858 to display the 106-carat Koh-I-Noor diamond, set in the front cross pattée and detachable. She also wears Queen Victoria's small crown and waterfall brooch.* OPPOSITE, BELOW LEFT: *Queen Mary is wearing the bar brooch with the 'Cambridge sapphires' – a parure of tiara, necklace, stomacher, earrings and two bracelets that the Duchess of Cambridge, Queen Mary's grandmother, gave to her eldest daughter Augusta in 1843 when she married the Grand Duke of Mecklenburg-Strelitz. The Grand Duchess left these on her death in 1916 to her niece and goddaughter, Queen Mary, who in turn gave them to her goddaughter Princess Marina of Greece when in 1934 she married Queen Mary's fourth son, the Duke of Kent. Part of the set is presently worn by the Duchess of Kent. (For the necklace in the parure see page 22, above right.)* OPPOSITE, CENTRE: *Queen Elizabeth the Queen Mother wearing the brooch for her official eightieth-birthday portrait in 1980. She has pinned it vertically instead of horizontally. Her diamond tiara was made in the 1940s but was slightly altered by Cartier in the early 1950s when the triangle motifs were added. The necklace is the one that Queen Alexandra was given for her wedding (page 92).* OPPOSITE, NEAR LEFT: *The Queen wore the brooch at the annual Ghillies Ball at Balmoral in 1972.*

Stomachers first became popular in the fifteenth century and were designed to cover the front of the bodice; as fashions changed, so did the shape of the stomacher. When the waistline disappeared altogether in the early 1920s, stomachers quickly sank into oblivion and were either divided into smaller, more wearable brooches, or the stones used for completely new pieces of jewellery. OPPOSITE: *Queen Mary gave this eight-inch-long Victorian stomacher to the Queen as a wedding gift in 1947. Designed as a series of intersecting circles and half circles, it has ten diamond drops, and divides horizontally into three separate brooches.* ABOVE, LEFT: *Queen Mary with King Albert and Queen Elizabeth of the Belgians in 1922, when she and the King were paying them a State visit. In addition to the stomacher, she is also wearing the diamond diadem that she had made in 1911 to wear at the Delhi Durbar. Originally there were cabochon emeralds set on top, but they had been removed by this date. In the front are the third and fourth Cullinan stones, which replace part of the original delicate scroll design. In 1947 Queen Mary lent the diadem to Queen Elizabeth for the official trip to South Africa, which included opening Parliament. The Cullinans had been removed and the original setting restored. That was the last occasion on which this tiara has been seen.* ABOVE, RIGHT: *The Queen in the Green Drawing Room at Buckingham Palace in 1953. She is wearing the bottom, smallest part of the stomacher only, and has never worn the complete brooch. Her early-nineteenth-century diamond fringe necklace, a traditional Russian design, is threaded on silk and was a wedding gift from the Lord Mayor and Aldermen of the City of London, the Governor of the Bank of England, the Chairmen of the Stock Exchange, Lloyds and the Baltic Exchange and the Committee of the Crown Clearing Banks.*

Queen Mary's Stomacher

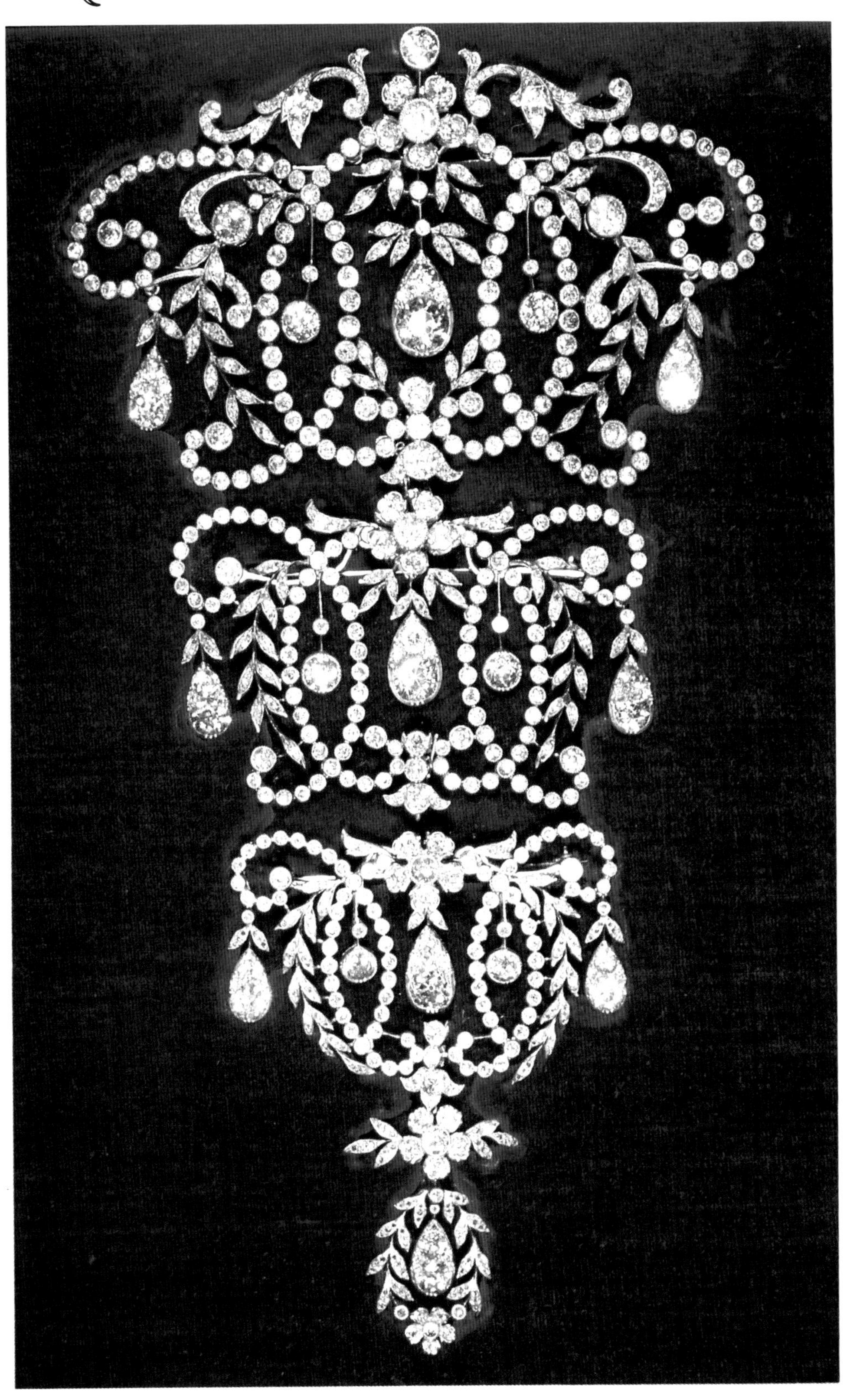

The King William IV Brooch

ABOVE: *In 1830 King William IV took six large brilliants and a number of smaller stones from a diamond-studded Badge of the Order of the Bath that had belonged to his father, King George III, and had this brooch made using the six large stones set in a circular frame around a cluster centre.* OPPOSITE, ABOVE LEFT: *This eleven-foot-high marble statue commemorates Queen Victoria's Golden Jubilee and was unveiled on 24 May 1889 at the Royal College of Physicians Examination Hall on the Embankment by the Prince of Wales, who in his speech said that there was 'nowhere a finer statue of the Queen'. The sculptor was Francis John Williamson. The brooch is pinned on her bodice just below the Crown collet necklace. In 1901 Queen Victoria left the brooch to the Crown.* OPPOSITE, ABOVE CENTRE: *Queen Alexandra wore the brooch in 1901 pinned at her waist.* OPPOSITE, ABOVE RIGHT: *Queen Mary in 1929 attached a large oval diamond drop to the brooch. Her diamond pear-shaped ring is the ninth Cullinan chip (page 84).* OPPOSITE, BELOW LEFT: *Queen Elizabeth the Queen Mother wore the brooch at her Coronation in 1937, and here in 1946 at the re-opening of the Royal Opera House Covent Garden after the war. Her diamond tiara of interconnecting circles originally belonged to Princess Mary Adelaide, Duchess of Teck, Queen Mary's mother, who wore it also as a necklace, as did Queen Elizabeth the Queen Mother (page 49). It now belongs to Princess Margaret, who only wears it as a necklace.* OPPOSITE, BELOW RIGHT: *The Queen in 1957 leading in her filly Carrozza after it won the Oaks.*

The Cullinan

Captain Frederick Wells, Superintendent of the Premier Mine, one of South Africa's most productive, which lies three hundred miles northeast of Kimberley in the Transvaal, was making his daily inspection on 25 January 1905, when he saw a flash of reflected light from the setting sun on the shaft wall. As he got closer to the spot, he detected a partially exposed crystal, which at first he thought must be a piece of broken glass planted there as a joke by one of the workers. Using his pocket-knife he finally dug out a rock that weighed 1⅓ lb and was 3⅞ inches long, 2¼ inches wide and 2⅝ inches high. Although it was twice the size of any diamond ever discovered and, so he believed, must surely be worthless, Wells was a professional and automatically sent his find to be analysed. His discovery turned out to be a diamond weighing 3,106 carats, and, because one side was smooth, the experts suggested that it was only part of a much larger stone that had been broken up by natural forces. Perfectly clear and colourless, it was immediately named after Sir Thomas M. Cullinan, Chairman of the Premier Diamond Company, who had discovered the mine in 1902 after a long period of fruitless prospecting in the area.

Captain Wells received a £3,500 reward for his find, and the Transvaal Government bought the stone for £150,000, although it was insured for ten times that amount. Understandably its discovery caused a world-wide sensation. The diamond's greatest value lay in the number of smaller gems that could be cut from it, and Prime Minister Botha proposed that the Cullinan be given to King Edward VII as a 'token of the loyalty and attachment of the people of Transvaal to his throne and person'. In the aftermath of the bitter Boer War, the diamond nearly became a political football when Parliament voted only forty-two to nineteen in favour of the presentation, oddly enough the Boers being for and the English settlers voting against. Sir Henry Campbell-Bannerman, the British Prime Minister, indecisively told the King that it must be his own decision as to whether he accepted or not after such a divided vote; but after persistent urging by Winston Churchill he finally agreed to accept it, and the Transvaal Government presented Churchill with a model of the diamond in gratitude, which he delighted in showing off to his friends, sometimes displaying it on a silver salver.

The last obstacle to be surmounted was that of safely transporting the stone to England. Detectives guarded the gem, insurance was arranged, and then it was packed up and sent off by ordinary parcel post while a fake stone was taken aboard a steamer under police escort and ceremoniously deposited in the Captain's safe, where it was guarded by detectives for the duration of the voyage. In England, on 9 November 1907, the King's sixty-sixth birthday, Sir Francis Hopwood and Mr Richard Solomon, Agent-General for the Transvaal in London, carrying the genuine stone with them, travelled by train to Sandringham in Norfolk, guarded by two senior Scotland Yard policemen. They reached the house safely, despite rumours of a planned robbery attempt. The presentation was made to the King while members of the large house party looked on, including the Queen of Spain, the Queen of Norway, Lord Revelstoke and Bendor Westminster. At lunch the conversation centred on how the stone ought to be cut so that it could be inserted in the Crown, and afterwards the King presented Solomon with the KCVO. The King announced, through the Secretary of State for the Colonies, Lord Elgin, that he accepted this magnificent gift 'for myself and successors' and said that he would arrange that 'this great and unique diamond be kept and preserved among the historic jewels which form the heirlooms of the Crown'.

King Edward took a great personal interest in the cutting of the Cullinan and the famous Dutch firm of Messrs I.J. Asscher of Amsterdam were entrusted with the task. They studied the stone for three months and then on 10 February 1908 at 2.45 pm, Joseph Asscher prepared to undertake the most momentous professional gamble he would ever make. He inserted his steel cleaving blade at the precise point they had agreed upon, and

with his heavy hammer gave one decisive blow. The stone didn't move, but the blade snapped. Mr Asscher calmly inserted a new blade and struck again. This time everything went according to plan and the diamond split in two, one piece weighing 1,977.5 carats, and the other, 1,040 carats. Amid the jubilation Mr Asscher slid quietly to the floor in a dead faint. Further cleaving produced nine major stones, known as the 'chips', ninety-six small brilliants and nearly 10 carats of unpolished 'ends'. The total weight amounted to 1,063 carats, which meant there had been a loss in cutting of 65 per cent. Later that year, Joseph Asscher and his brother, Louis, travelled to England and gave the King the two principal stones. It had been previously agreed that all the rest would stay with the Asschers as their fee for the job, but King Edward now purchased the sixth Cullinan 'chip', an 11.5-carat marquise-cut stone and gave it to Queen Alexandra as a present. The King called the four largest stones the Stars of Africa. The Cullinan I, a 530.2-carat pear-shaped stone, 2⅛ inches long, 1¾ inches wide and one inch thick at its deepest point, and the Cullinan II, an oblong of 317.4 carats, were sent to the Tower of London to be displayed with the rest of the Crown Jewels, as well as the hammer and cleaver with which Joseph Asscher had shaped them. They are the two largest cut stones in the world. A brooch and pendant setting were produced so that Queen Alexandra could wear them pinned to her Garter sash for the annual Opening of Parliament, but otherwise they remained on public display. Garrard, the crown jeweller, was instructed to use the Cullinans I and II for the Coronation of King George V on 22 June 1911.

Cullinan I, now always called the Greater Star of Africa, was set in the head of the Sceptre with the Cross, and Cullinan II was mounted at the front of the brow band of the Imperial State Crown.

In 1910 Prime Minister Botha insisted that all the other stones cut from the Cullinan be purchased by the South African Government from Asschers as he feared they might be bought by private individuals. They were to be given to Queen Mary, then the Princess of Wales, during a visit she was to make that year with her husband to open the South African Parliament. However, their tour was cancelled because of King Edward VII's death and, instead, they were presented to her at Marlborough House on 28 June 1910 by Sir Richard Solomon, then High Commissioner of the Union of South Africa – the same man who had given the uncut stone to King Edward three years earlier.

PAGE 83: *The Cullinan III and Cullinan IV, known as the Lesser Stars of Africa, were set as a brooch by Queen Mary in 1910. It is the single most valuable item owned by the Queen, who inherited the pieces of jewellery made from the Cullinan cleavings on the death of her grandmother in 1953. The pear-drop (III) of 94.4 carats hangs from (IV) a square-cut stone of 63.6 carats.* ABOVE: *Queen Mary set the ninth Cullinan chip, a 4.4-carat pear-shaped stone, in a ring with a claw setting. (She is seen wearing it in the photograph on page 81.)* OPPOSITE, LEFT: *Queen Mary on 6 February 1911. Dressed in full mourning for King Edward VII, King George V had opened Parliament for the first time, and he and the Queen posed for the first official photographs of their reign. The Queen is wearing Queen Victoria's Koh-I-Noor diadem, earrings and her two large bow brooches in addition to the Crown collet necklace, from which she has removed the drop and substituted the Lesser Stars of Africa as a pendant. Pinned to her Garter sash are the Crown Jewels, Cullinans I and II, worn as a brooch, and she is wearing seven rows of diamonds as a collar. Queen Mary wore the Lesser Stars of Africa brooch on all important occasions, including the marriages of four of her children and the wedding of Princess Elizabeth in 1947. She would also hang the Cullinan I as a pendant from*

The Lesser Stars of Africa Brooch and The Cullinan IX Ring

the Koh-I-Noor brooch. For her Coronation in 1911, she had Cullinan III placed in the surmounting cross of her new crown, and Cullinan IV was set on the circlet; this is the only occasion when they appeared as part of the Crown Regalia. ABOVE, RIGHT: *In comparison to Cullinans I and II, it is perhaps understandable that Queen Mary used to refer to her Lesser Stars of Africa as the 'chips', and from this comes one of the most misapplied quotations of the present Queen's reign. On 25 March 1958, while on a State visit to Holland, the Queen and Prince Philip made a tour of the Asscher diamond works, and, in talking about the cutting of the Cullinan diamond fifty years earlier, she referred to the Cullinans III and IV, which were pinned to her lapel, as 'Granny's Chips'. It is these two stones alone that are so nicknamed. This was one of the first occasions on which the Queen had ever worn the brooch, and during the afternoon she unpinned it and handed it to Louis Asscher who had been a witness as his brother cleaved the stone. The elderly man, nearly blind, was deeply moved that Her Majesty had brought the Cullinans with her, knowing how much it would mean to him to see them again after all these years. The Queen has worn the brooch perhaps no more than six times during her reign, but she wore it for this 1985 portrait as well as the ring made from the Cullinan IX chip.*

THE CULLINAN V HEART BROOCH

ABOVE, RIGHT: *At the time Queen Mary was given the 102 Cullinan cleavings in 1910, she had no idea that she was about to acquire the Cambridge emeralds, which came into her possession later that same year. This brooch, made to show off the Cullinan V, an 18.8-carat heart-shaped stone, then became the centre of a massive diamond and emerald stomacher, the pieces coming apart to be worn as separate brooches (page 52, above left). The heart-shaped platinum setting and the positioning of the collets in the brooch were all expressly designed to accentuate the shape of the stone. Queen Mary wore the brooch alone in 1911 pinned to the simple daytime dresses she wore aboard ship as she and the King travelled to India for the Delhi Durbar. It was on her toque hat during the 1935 Silver Jubilee service held in St Paul's Cathedral, and for the Coronation of her son King George VI in 1937 she wore the circlet portion of her own 1911 crown with this brooch inserted as the centrepiece of the front cross pattée.* ABOVE: *In 1926 Queen Mary wore the heart-shaped Cullinan V and attached to it the brooch made from the Cullinan VII and Cullinan VIII chips.* RIGHT: *Of all the Queen's jewellery, this is one of the brooches she wears most often, as here on a trip to Australia in 1963.*

THE CULLINAN VII AND CULLINAN VIII BROOCH

ABOVE: *Queen Mary used the Cullinan VII, an 8.8-carat marquise-cut stone, as a pendant to the Cullinan VIII, a 6.8-carat oblong brilliant, to form a second brooch, made at the same time as the Cullinan heart brooch and very similar in design.* ABOVE, RIGHT: *Queen Mary photographed with her only daughter, Princess Mary, later the Princess Royal, in VAD uniform, at Buckingham Palace in 1919. Queen Mary's platinum and diamond pendant and chain has some of the ninety-six smaller Cullinan cleavings in it, and was inherited by the Queen in 1953. She has never worn it in public, complaining that 'it gets in the soup'.* RIGHT: *The Queen and Prince Philip on their 1961 trip to Sierra Leone. Notice how Queen Mary always wore her brooches dead centre, while the Queen invariably pins her brooches on her left shoulder.*

QUEEN ELIZABETH THE QUEEN MOTHER'S LEAF BROOCH

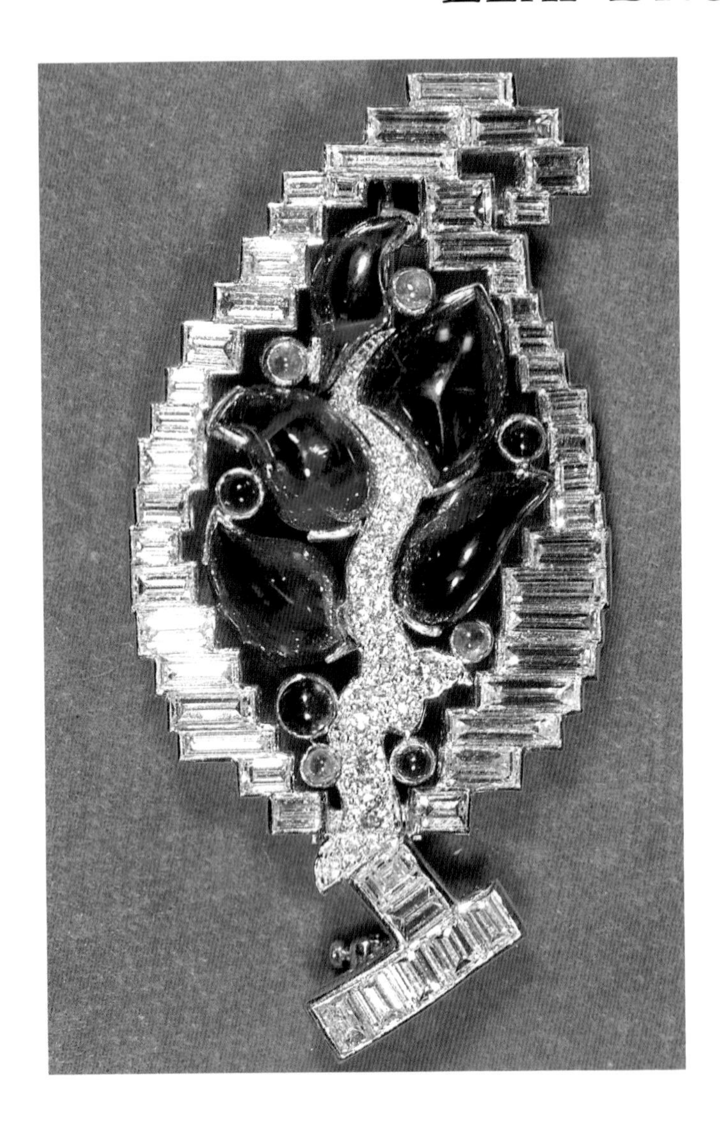

ABOVE: *Framed in diamond baguettes, this Cartier leaf-shaped brooch has a pavé-set diamond vein down the centre, and is set with irregularly shaped Indian-cut Ceylonese cabochon sapphires, and small round emeralds, amethysts and a ruby. The Duke of York bought it for his wife in 1928.* ABOVE, RIGHT: *Queen Elizabeth the Queen Mother, then Duchess of York, wore it pinned to her velvet cloche hat in 1930.* RIGHT: *She gave it to her daughter as a wartime birthday gift, and twenty-year-old Princess Elizabeth wore it on her lapel during a visit to Nottingham in 1946.*

The Queen's Flower Spray Brooch

The Queen's Set of Flower Clips

ABOVE, LEFT: *A Cartier gold spray brooch with one flower of all blue sapphires and another of pink sapphires and cushion-cut rubies. Both have square-cut diamond centres and one of the three leaves is set with pavé-set diamonds. It was a birthday gift to the Queen from her parents in 1945 together with a matching pair of earrings in the shape of miniature flowers on tiny stems.* LEFT: *For her twenty-third birthday, on 21 April 1949, the first photograph was released of the Duke and Duchess of Edinburgh with Prince Charles.*

ABOVE: *The Queen's Cartier gold flower clips, with clusters of cushion-shaped sapphires and brilliant-cut diamonds in their centres, were bought separately in 1942 and 1944 by King George and Queen Elizabeth. Princess Margaret was given an identical set, but with ruby clusters. She sold hers some years ago at Christie's.* RIGHT: *Princess Elizabeth on her first visit to Washington in 1951.*

The Queen's

Jardinière Brooch Flower Basket Brooch

ABOVE, LEFT: *This small Art Deco platinum and diamond basket brooch overflowing with cabochon ruby berries, carved pale Indian emerald leaves and sapphire flowers, was a typical design of the 1930s, and variations of it were produced by Cartier in large numbers.* LEFT: *It was a present to the Queen from her parents in 1941, and she wears it here bicycling at Royal Lodge, Windsor, on 11 April 1942.*

ABOVE, RIGHT: *Bigger and more sophisticated than the jardinière brooch, this has a more naturalistic design with its simple garden-basket shape and spray of ruby, diamond and sapphire flowers. This style of brooch was sometimes known as a* giardinetti *– 'little flower garden'. It was given to the Queen in November 1948 by her parents to mark the birth of Prince Charles, and she wore it a month later for his first official photographs.* RIGHT: *The Queen in 1973.*

Queen Elizabeth the Queen Mother's Flower Brooch

LEFT: *In the late 1930s, Queen Elizabeth wore this five-petalled flower brooch with a cluster centre. She is seen here with her two daughters in 1936.* BELOW: *The Queen, then Princess Elizabeth, borrowed the brooch from her mother on a number of occasions and wore it at the International Horse Trials, at Badminton, in 1953. Princess Margaret is pictured on her left.*

QUEEN ALEXANDRA'S TRIPLE DROP BROOCH

ABOVE: *Photographed in its original velvet case, this is the suite of jewellery made by Garrard and given to Princess Alexandra by the Prince of Wales as a wedding present in 1863, and which she wore on her wedding day. The necklace has eight circular clusters of diamonds with a large pearl in the centre of each, connected by festoons of diamonds. From each of the three front clusters hangs a pear-shaped pearl. The matching earrings are owned by the Queen today (page 34), but the oblong diamond brooch, set with three pearls and with three detachable pendant pearls suspended from single large diamonds, and the necklace have belonged to Queen Elizabeth the Queen Mother since the accession of King George VI in 1936.* OPPOSITE, ABOVE LEFT: *Princess Alexandra wearing the brooch, around 1896. Her diamond tiara, consisting of a three-row circlet surmounted by scroll ornaments (which could be connected by Greek devices, but not seen here), was also a wedding gift from the Prince of Wales, and could be dismantled and worn as a number of different ornaments. The bottom diamond necklace, which she wore at her Coronation in 1902, also comes apart, and is the one that was strung in separate sections from Queen Victoria's bow brooches down the length of her skirt (page 67).* OPPOSITE, ABOVE RIGHT: *Queen Mary wore the oblong brooch, without the pearl pendants, pinned on the side of her bodice in 1938. The round pearl surrounded by a circle of diamonds pinned above her stomacher is the brooch Queen Victoria wore with her Golden Jubilee necklace (page 40).* OPPOSITE, BELOW LEFT: *Queen Mary arriving at St Paul's Cathedral on 26 April 1948 for the service to celebrate the Silver Wedding of King George VI and Queen Elizabeth. She is wearing the brooch complete with its pendant drops.* OPPOSITE, BELOW RIGHT: *In 1972 the Queen wore the brooch at an official reception during her State visit to France. This is the only time she has ever worn it.*

WESTMINSTER
LIMITED

Queen Mary's Three Leaf Clover Bar Brooch

Queen Mary owned this unusual brooch, a large round pearl crossed by a curved diamond bar that ends in two three-leaf clovers, as early as 1931 when she posed for a formal photograph with the five-year-old Princess Elizabeth. ABOVE, LEFT: *Queen Mary wearing the brooch in 1948. The jewelled enamel buckle clasp on her coat and her parasol handle were both made by Fabergé.* ABOVE, RIGHT: *The Queen inherited the brooch in 1953, but wore it for the first time in public at the 1985 Windsor Horse Show.*

Queen Mary's 'Women of Hampshire' Harebell Pendant Brooch

ABOVE: *In 1893, the 'Women of Hampshire' committee, led by the Duchess of Wellington, collected £775 to buy a wedding gift for Princess May of Teck. The Duchess assembled a number of items at her London home, Apsley House, and a representative group travelled up from Hampshire to make their choice. They selected a fine diamond pendant with a pear-shaped pearl drop. In her thank-you letter dated 4 July 1893, Princess May asked the Duchess to 'please tell them how grateful I am for the beautiful diamond and pearl pendant, which I shall often wear.' By 1911 the pendant had been converted into a brooch.* ABOVE, LEFT: *Queen Mary wearing the brooch in 1948.* ABOVE, RIGHT: *The Queen inherited the brooch in 1953 and wears it here on a visit to Guernsey in 1957.*

The Duchess of Teck's Corsage Brooch

ABOVE, RIGHT: *This corsage jewel is typically Victorian in execution, designed to be big and impressive, but less grand than a stomacher. The brooch consists of a large pearl set in a circle of diamonds enclosed in a diamond-plaited scroll frame with twelve further collet stones set around the edge. A U-shaped chain of larger collet diamonds ends in three pendant pearl drops.* ABOVE, LEFT: *Princess Mary Adelaide, Duchess of Teck, wearing the brooch, around 1895. It was inherited in 1897 by her daughter, the future Queen Mary, who gave it to the Queen as a wedding gift in 1947.* LEFT: *The Queen wore the brooch as she arrived in Nepal in 1961.*

The Duchess of Cambridge's Pendant Brooch

RIGHT: *A baroque pearl in a diamond-set mount hangs from a diamond pendant below a large round pearl framed by fourteen brilliant-cut diamonds.* BELOW, LEFT: *The brooch belonged to Queen Mary's grandmother, Princess Augusta, Duchess of Cambridge, who was painted wearing it by Heinrich von Angeli, in 1877. When she died at the age of ninety-one, on 6 April 1889, at York House, St James's Palace, the brooch was inherited by her younger daughter, Princess Mary Adelaide, Duchess of Teck. She died intestate in 1897 and her jewellery was divided among her four children, this brooch being part of Queen Mary's portion.* BELOW, CENTRE: *It was one of her favourite brooches and she wore it constantly for the rest of her life. With her passion for family history, it must have pleased Queen Mary to wear her grandmother's brooch at the christening of her great-grandson, and godson, Prince Charles, in the Music Room at Buckingham Palace on 15 December 1948. She had also worn it for his mother's christening, the present Queen, in 1926.* BELOW, RIGHT: *The Queen inherited it in 1953 and wore it at Windsor Castle on her forty-eighth birthday on 21 April 1974. Despite the deceptive simplicity of its design, at a Buckingham Palace garden party in 1985, the brooch, pinned to the left shoulder of Her Majesty's pale blue silk long-sleeved dress, was so large that it was easily picked out as the Queen moved slowly through the crowd of eight thousand people.*

The Prince Albert Brooch

ABOVE: *This magnificent brooch, a large oblong sapphire surrounded by twelve round diamonds, was given to Queen Victoria by Prince Albert of Saxe-Coburg-Gotha on Sunday, 9 February 1840, at Buckingham Palace. It was the day before their wedding and she noted in her diary that, after a religious service in the Bow Room, 'dearest Albert' came upstairs to her sitting room and gave her four fans and a 'beautiful sapphire and diamond brooch'. For their wedding in the Chapel Royal, St James's Palace, she wore it with her Turkish diamond necklace and earrings.* OPPOSITE, ABOVE LEFT: *While Prince Albert was alive the Queen wore it constantly, as here in an 1843 lithograph – which in 1851 she arranged to have produced cheaply enough so that even the poorer of her subjects could afford to buy it. During her forty years of widowhood, however, she was rarely seen wearing the brooch. In her will she instructed that it was to be considered a Crown piece of jewellery and held in trust for all future Queens of Great Britain. Her two bar brooches were remade as the double bar brooch (page 77).* OPPOSITE, ABOVE RIGHT: *Queen Alexandra wore the Prince Albert brooch pinned on the right of her bodice for her Coronation in 1902.* OPPOSITE, BELOW LEFT: *Queen Mary often wore it in the daytime, as seen here in 1927, with matching earrings.* OPPOSITE, CENTRE: *Queen Elizabeth the Queen Mother, who wore the brooch only occasionally during the war years, did so at the 1942 christening of Prince William of Gloucester. It came to the Queen on her accession.* OPPOSITE, BELOW RIGHT: *The Queen in July 1972, at the launch of a RNLI lifeboat.*

THE EMPRESS MARIE FEODOROVNA OF RUSSIA'S BROOCH

ABOVE: *A cabochon sapphire brooch surrounded by two rows of diamonds with a pearl drop hanging from a collet diamond. The brooch was a wedding gift in 1866 to Princess Dagmar of Denmark, on her marriage to the Tsarevich Alexander, from her sister and brother-in-law the Prince and Princess of Wales.* OPPOSITE, ABOVE LEFT: *Queen Alexandra, Empress Marie and their youngest sister, Thyra, the Duchess of Cumberland, playing cards with their father, King Christian IX, at the Palace in Copenhagen in April 1905. The Empress, who is seated on King Christian's right, is wearing the brooch pinned on her bodice.* OPPOSITE, ABOVE RIGHT: *Queen Mary purchased the brooch from the Dowager Empress Marie's estate in 1929. She wears it here in 1938.* OPPOSITE, BELOW: *The Queen inherited the brooch in 1953, and wears it while visiting the Solomon Islands in 1982.*

QUEEN MARY'S RUSSIAN BROOCH

The Queen's Eighteenth Birthday Bracelet

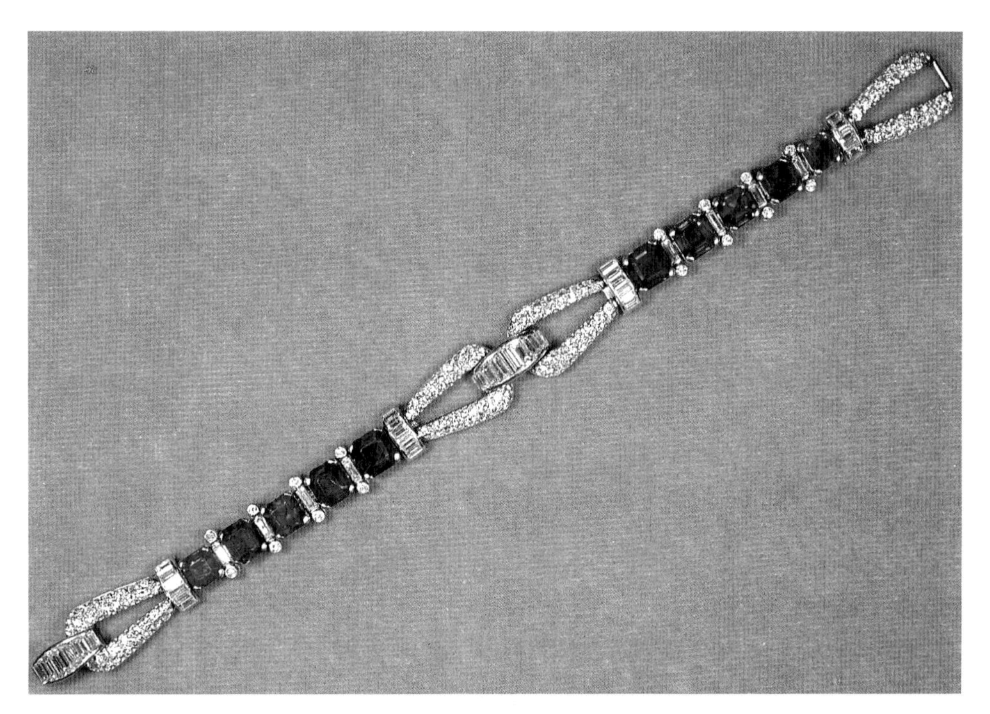

OPPOSITE, ABOVE: *Queen Alexandra's sister, the Empress Marie Feodorovna of Russia, gave Princess May of Teck this unusual brooch of a large square-cut diamond and a square cabochon sapphire set in a scroll frame of round diamonds as a wedding present in 1893. The Empress and her husband, Tsar Alexander III, later added sapphire and diamond bracelets to the gift.* OPPOSITE, BELOW RIGHT: *In 1925 Queen Mary pinned the brooch horizontally on her collar.* OPPOSITE, BELOW LEFT: *In 1974 the Queen, who had inherited the brooch in 1953, wore it pinned vertically on her shoulder.* ABOVE: *For her eighteenth birthday, in 1944, the King gave Princess Elizabeth this unusual Cartier linked bracelet of square-cut sapphires interspersed with baguette diamonds and ending in diamond loops joined by arcs of baguette diamonds.* RIGHT: *The Queen and Prince Philip leaving the theatre in 1955.*

THE QUEEN'S CARTIER CLIPS

ABOVE: *The idea of clip brooches came to French jeweller Louis Cartier as he idly watched a peasant woman hanging out her washing with wooden clothes pegs, and he popularized his idea in the 1930s by designing brooches so that they could be worn as a single brooch or as two matching clips. These aquamarine and diamond clips were given to the Queen in 1944 by her parents as an eighteenth-birthday present, and are a typically 1940s design, combining baguette, oval and round stones.* ABOVE, RIGHT: *In 1958 the Queen wore them as separate clips.* RIGHT: *In 1965, as she and Prince Philip attended Royal Ascot, the Queen wore them as a brooch. The Royal Meeting at Ascot, a racecourse founded by Queen Anne in 1711 on land close to Windsor Castle, is held annually in the third week of June. The Ascot racecourse still belongs to the Monarch.*

Queen Mary's Link Bracelet

ABOVE, LEFT: *In 1929 Queen Mary purchased from the estate of the Dowager Empress Marie Feodorovna of Russia this diamond tiara with a large sapphire mounted in the front scallop, sapphire and diamond cluster earrings, the diamond chain-link choker necklace, and the brooch of a square-cut sapphire surrounded by two rows of diamonds. She is wearing them for her official sixty-ninth birthday photograph in 1936. The sapphire surrounded by brilliant-cut diamonds in the tiara was removable and either a diamond flower matching the side motifs or a pink beryl could be worn in its place. Queen Mary gave the sapphire to Princess Margaret to be worn as a brooch, and the tiara to her daughter-in-law, Princess Alice, Duchess of Gloucester, who now shares it with her daughter-in-law, the present Duchess. The brooch was left to the Queen, but is not used. The earrings were left to Princess Marina, who left them to the Duchess of Kent.* ABOVE, RIGHT: *The diamond chain-link necklace could be divided into two bracelets, which is how Queen Mary wore it for her official birthday photograph in 1938. The Koh-I-Noor diamond, which is Crown property, had been removed from the front cross pattée of the diamond circlet, and given to Queen Elizabeth to wear in the new crown made for her Coronation in 1937, and Queen Mary has replaced it with the Cullinan V heart brooch.* LEFT: *The Queen wearing the bracelet which she inherited from Queen Mary in 1953. On her left wrist is a diamond evening watch with an oblong face and bracelet strap that she has had since the late 1940s.*

OPPOSITE: *Queen Mary first went to India as Princess of Wales in 1905 and instantly fell in love with the country. 'Lovely India, beautiful India', she said repeatedly. In 1907 the Maharajah of Bikaner presented her with these typically Indian twin diamond-studded bangles, which can either be worn separately or, when a hidden hinge is snapped, as one.* ABOVE, LEFT: *Queen Mary in 1911 wearing the bracelets on her left wrist.* ABOVE, RIGHT: *In 1947 Queen Mary gave them as a wedding gift to Princess Elizabeth, who wore them in 1951 to a dinner given by King Haakon of Norway who was in London on a State visit. Her diamond bandeau tiara was made by Cartier, Paris, in a wreath design of English roses and foliage, a style typical of the early nineteenth century. The central large rose and the two slightly smaller side ones were detachable and could be worn independently as brooches. The piece was a wedding gift from the Nizam of Hyderabad and Berar, who himself possessed one of the world's most valuable jewellery collections. Although the Queen continues to wear the brooches – the large rose on its own, the smaller two together – the tiara was broken up and the diamonds used for the new ruby and diamond tiara she had made in 1973 (page 70). The diamond flower-petal earrings were a twenty-first-birthday present from the Diplomatic Corps.*

Queen Mary's Indian Bangle Bracelets

The Queen's Modern Baguettes and Brilliants Bracelet

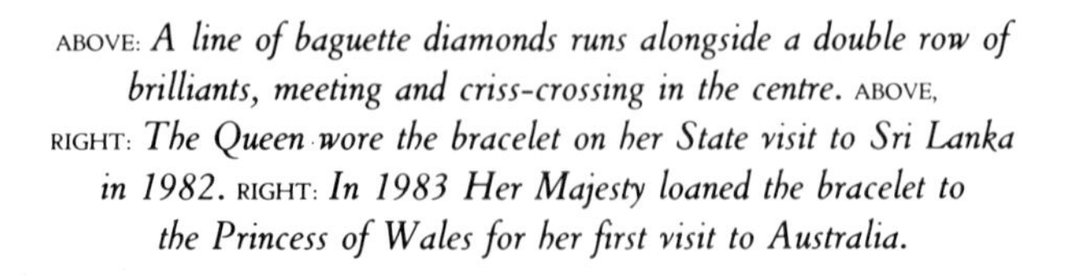

ABOVE: *A line of baguette diamonds runs alongside a double row of brilliants, meeting and criss-crossing in the centre.* ABOVE, RIGHT: *The Queen wore the bracelet on her State visit to Sri Lanka in 1982.* RIGHT: *In 1983 Her Majesty loaned the bracelet to the Princess of Wales for her first visit to Australia.*

THE QUEEN'S ENGAGEMENT RING AND THE PRINCE PHILIP WEDDING BRACELET

ABOVE, LEFT: *The diamonds in the Queen's engagement ring and her wedding present from Prince Philip, a bracelet, all came from a tiara that belonged to his mother, Princess Andrew of Greece. Her brother, Earl Mountbatten of Burma, loved to design jewellery for his wife and he had often used the London firm of Philip Antrobus Ltd, which was founded in Birmingham in 1815. He recommended them to his nephew, who also had very strong views on design and knew what he wanted done. Antrobus dismantled the tiara, and the platinum ring was set with eleven diamonds, a central solitaire stone of 3 carats with five smaller stones set in each shoulder. The ring was made by George Taubl, and the stones set by Harry Marchant. Prince Philip formally asked the King's permission to marry his daughter on 8 July 1947, he then produced the ring, but unfortunately it was discovered to be slightly too big and had to be sent back to Antrobus to be made smaller. However, the ring was returned in time for the Princess to wear it on 10 July, after the engagement was formally announced and the couple posed for photographers. That afternoon at a Buckingham Palace garden party the guests crowded around to get their first look at the ring. To this day, if the Queen is annoyed about anything, she will start to twist the ring round and round, a sign that her staff recognizes immediately.* ABOVE: *Prince Philip was also deeply involved with the design of the wide diamond and platinum bracelet that he gave to the Queen as his wedding gift. She wears it often at night or when in full ceremonial dress for a public event such as the Opening of Parliament.* LEFT: *The Queen in 1948.*

Queen Alexandra's Bracelet

ABOVE: *For her Coronation on 9 August 1902, Queen Alexandra wore on her left wrist a four-row pearl bracelet with a large sapphire and diamond clasp. The pearls may have been the eighty-eight that were made into a bracelet by Queen Victoria in 1838, and left to the Crown. This photograph is of particular historical interest because, compared with most other pictures of Queen Alexandra, it was never retouched, and so gives us the rare opportunity of seeing exactly what she looked like at the age of fifty-eight.* RIGHT: *The Queen wearing the bracelet on a visit to New Zealand in 1954.*

THE KING WILLIAM IV BUCKLE BRACELETS

THE ILLUSTRATED LONDON NEWS,

No. 3921.—VOL. CXLIV. SATURDAY, JUNE 13, 1914. With Summer Season and Special Supplement. ONE SHILLING.

THE FIRST NATURAL-COLOUR PHOTOGRAPH OF THE QUEEN PUBLISHED IN THE "ILLUSTRATED LONDON NEWS" BY SPECIAL PERMISSION: HER MAJESTY

On King George V's accession to the Throne in 1910, Queen Mary had two blue enamel buckle mounts set as the centrepieces of matching four-row diamond bracelets, one of which was made in 1838 and left to the Crown by Queen Victoria; the other, which had formerly had a large portrait medallion of Prince Albert, was worn by Queen Victoria every day of her life following her marriage. The buckles had originally belonged to King William IV, and are surrounded by two rows of brilliant-cut diamonds with his cypher of WR surmounted by a crown on one, and that of Queen Adelaide on the other.

RIGHT: *Queen Mary wore them at her Coronation in 1911, and here in 1914. She is also wearing the circlet part of her crown with the 106-carat Koh-I-Noor diamond set above Cullinan IV. Cullinans I and II are worn as a brooch, and Cullinan III as a pendant from Queen Victoria's collet necklace.* ABOVE, LEFT: *In 1937 Queen Mary gave the bracelets to Queen Elizabeth and she too wore them at her Coronation. She wears them here in 1947, at a reception at County Hall. They became the property of the Queen in 1952.* ABOVE, RIGHT: *The Queen wore them at a 1953 reception to celebrate her Coronation, also at County Hall.*

Queen Mary's Bracelet

ABOVE: *For her official 1935 Silver Jubilee photograph, Queen Mary wore on her right wrist a five-row pearl bracelet that has a large, oval, diamond-cluster clasp.*
LEFT: *The Queen inherited the bracelet in 1953 and wears it here in 1956.*

Princess Marie Louise's Bracelet

ABOVE: *Princess Marie Louise was the younger daughter of Queen Victoria's third daughter, Princess Helena, and Prince Christian of Schleswig-Holstein. She was born in 1872 and died in 1956 at the age of eighty-four. Known to the Queen as 'Cousin Louie', she was an endless source of family anecdotes, and it was her idea to create Queen Mary's Dolls' House, now on display at Windsor Castle. She left one of the two pearl and diamond honeycomb bracelets on her left wrist to the Queen and the diamond brooch on her bodice to Queen Elizabeth the Queen Mother. She is photographed here two years before her death.* LEFT: *The Queen wearing the bracelet at a banquet given by King Faisal of Saudi Arabia at the Dorchester Hotel in 1967. The King had given Her Majesty her diamond necklace two days earlier* *(page 46)*.

Queen Mary's Rose of York Bracelet

OPPOSITE: *When she married the Duke of York in 1893 Princess May of Teck was given a number of jewels in the shape of the Rose of York. One such, from the Duke of York himself, was a ruby and diamond pendant with a square ruby centre. Queen Mary gave it to Princess Elizabeth in 1947 as a wedding present, set as the centrepiece of a gold cuff bracelet with bands of ruby and diamond leaves on either side.* ABOVE, LEFT: *In 1898 Queen Mary, then Duchess of York, had removed the diamond-studded pendant loop, and wore it as a brooch on her high stiff collar when photographed here with her two oldest sons, the future Kings Edward VIII and George VI.* ABOVE, RIGHT: *In May 1951, the Queen wore the bracelet together with another wedding gift, a Cartier platinum and diamond necklace and pendant designed to represent English roses and foliage, given to her by the Nizam of Hyderabad and Berar.*

The Queen's Fifth Wedding Anniversary Bracelet

ABOVE: *Over the years, Prince Philip has designed a number of gifts for the Queen. This bracelet, made by Boucheron, was to celebrate their fifth wedding anniversary in 1952. It has gold links in the shape of interlocked E's and P's, and the centre medallion is Prince Philip's naval badge set in diamonds. There are two sapphire baguette crosses, a ruby cross, and two ruby and diamond studded flowers with fluted petals.*
LEFT: *The Queen wearing the bracelet, as she and Prince Philip arrived at Royal Ascot, in 1954.*

QUEEN ELIZABETH THE QUEEN MOTHER'S QUARTET OF BRACELETS

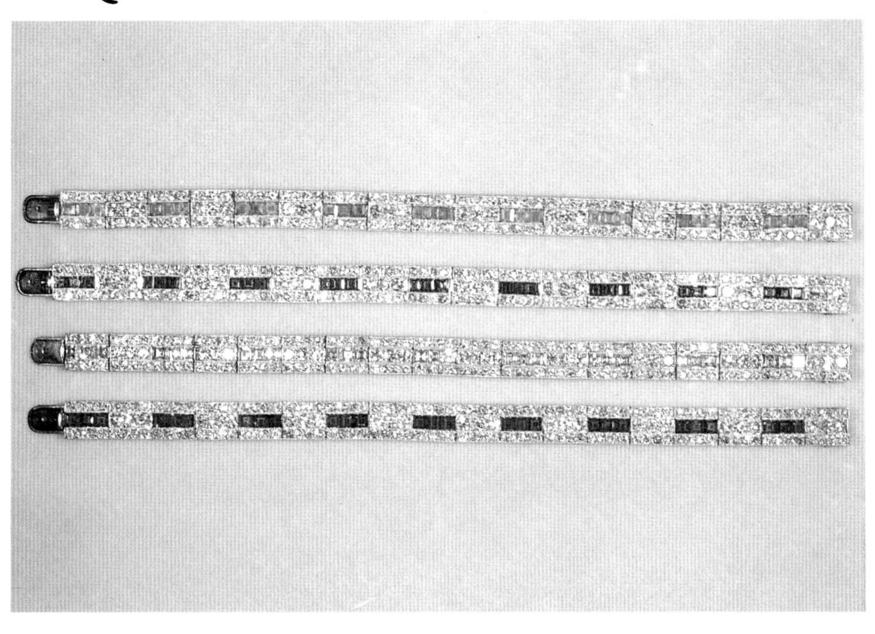

ABOVE: *These four matching Cartier diamond-strip bracelets have different baguette centres: sapphire, emerald, ruby and diamond.* ABOVE, RIGHT: *The Duke of York, later King George VI, bought them separately as gifts for his wife in 1924 and 1925. The Duchess of York, now Queen Elizabeth the Queen Mother, wearing all four in 1929. Her diamond fan-motif tiara, worn in the style of the day across her forehead, now belongs to Princess Margaret. Her Victorian turquoise and diamond brooch, and the matching earrings worn as pendant drops on her ropes of pearls, were part of a suite she received as a wedding gift from King George V in 1923, and which now also belong to Princess Margaret.* RIGHT: *The Queen wearing the diamond and ruby bracelets at a Variety Performance in Windsor for her Silver Jubilee in 1977.*

Queen Mary's Art Deco Bracelet

LEFT: *Queen Mary later added this wide diamond bracelet set with two square emeralds to the Cambridge and Delhi Durbar parure, and wore it for her Silver Jubilee portrait in 1935.* BELOW: *The Queen and Prince Philip arriving at Royal Ascot in 1967.*

The Swiss Federal Republic's Watch

ABOVE: *The Swiss Federal Republic presented this specially designed platinum watch to the Queen in 1947 as a wedding gift. It was made at Vacheron & Constantin, the world's oldest watch factory, founded in Geneva in 1785. The diamond-encircled round watch face is joined to the diamond-set strap with loops of diamonds.* ABOVE, RIGHT: *The Queen wore the watch to a reception in 1975.* RIGHT: *In 1981 the Queen gave the watch to the Princess of Wales as a wedding gift. She wears it here in 1983, leaving a film premiere with Prince Charles. Her engagement ring is a large oval sapphire surrounded by fourteen round diamonds and set in 18-carat white gold.*

PHOTOGRAPH CREDITS

The author and publisher would like to thank the following for permission to reproduce illustrations and for supplying photographs.

The following photographs are reproduced by gracious permission of HER MAJESTY QUEEN ELIZABETH II. Copyright reserved, 11, 12, 14, 18 above, 21, 40 below, 44, 50, 54 above left, 58 above, 70 above left. The following photographs are reproduced by gracious permission of HER MAJESTY QUEEN ELIZABETH II. Copyright reserved. Photographs by Maurice Foster, 4, 18 below, 26 above, 27 above left, above right, 28, 30, 32 above left, 34 above, 38 above left, above right, 39 centre, 40 above centre, 42 below, 46 above, 48, 52 above centre, below centre, 62 above, 66, 68 above, 70 above right, 72 above, 74 above, 75 left, 77, 79, 80, 83, 84, 86 above right, 87 above left, 88 above left, 89 above left, above right, 90 above left, above right, 95 below, 97 above, 98, 101, 102 above, 103 above, 104 left, 107, 108 left, 109 above left, above right, 114, 116 above, 117 above left.

Marcus Adams, 54 below left, 56 right; Marcus Adams/Popperfoto, 55 above right; Associated Press, 31 below right, 74 below, 89 below right, 95 above left; Baron/Camera Press, 51 left, 58 below, 62 below, 72 below right, 78 right, 89 below left; Bassano & Vandyk, 81 above right, 112 right; BBC Hulton Picture Library, 13 above left, above right, 15 above left, 19 above left, 22 above left, above right, below left, 24 right, 31 above left, above right, 32 above right, below left, below right, 33, 34 below left, 37 above left, above right, 39 left, 40 above left, above right, 42 above left, above right, 45 above left, above right, 46 below right, 49, 52 above left, above right, 54 above centre, 60 above left, below right, 65 above left, 67 above left, above centre, above right, 69 above left, 72 below left, 73 left, 75 above left, 76 above left, above right, below left, 81 above centre, below right, 85 left, 86 above right, 88 above right, 90 below left, 92, 93 above left, below right, 97 below centre, 99 above left, above right, below left, below centre, 100 above right, 102 below left, below right, 104 below right, 106 left, 110 left, 112 left, 113 right, 115 left, 118 below, 119 above right; Cecil Beaton, 45 below left, Cecil Beaton/Camera Press, 71; BIPPA, 26 below left, 37 below, 60 below left, 73 right, 93 below left, 64 above; Anthony Buckley/Camera Press, 19 below, 105 below; Camera Press, 16 right, 52 below left; Colorific, 94 right; Courtauld Institute of Art, 81 above left; Daily Sketch, 45 below right, 77 below right; General Photographic Agency, 15 below; Tim Graham, 16 left, 26 below right, 47 left, 108 above right, 119 below; Anwar Hussein, 46 below left, 53 right, 67 below right; Karsh/Camera Press, 85 right, 115 right; Lafeyette, 53 left; Serge Lemoine/BBC Hulton Picture Library, 61; Patrick Lichfield/Camera Press, 76 below centre; London News Agency, 94 left; Donald McKague/Camera Press, 25; Mansell Collection, 36, 91 above, 100 above left, 111 below, 117 above right; National Portrait Gallery, London, 55 above left; Desmond O'Neill, 64 below; Norman Parkinson/Camera Press, 54 above right, 76 below right; Pathe Gazette, 65 above right; Photographic News Agencies, 27 below, 35, 104 above right; The Photo Source, 4, 20 above right, 31 below left, 38 below, 43, 56 left, 69 above right, 86 below, 91 below, 99 below right; Planet News Ltd, 81 below left, 88 below right, 116 below; Popperfoto, 13 below left, 15 above right, 19 above right, 22 below right, 51 right, 60 above right, 78 left, 105 above left, above right, 106 right, 118 above; Press Association, 13 below right, 17, 20 below, 47 right, 59 left, 63, 97 below right, 113 left, 117 below; Pricam, 119 above left; Reuter/Press Association, 23 above, 54 below right, 87 above right, 95 above right, 103 below, 109 below, 110 right; John Shelley, 59 right, 65 below, 69 below, 70 below right; Soper, 93 above right; Sport and General, 20 above left, 52 below right, 67 below left; Syndication International, 90 below right; The Times, 29 right; Topham, 111 above right.